An Honorable Journey
In Search of Truth

BOB ALBA

ISBN: 978-1-09831-910-6 (print)
ISBN: 978-1-09831-911-3 (ebook)

Here's to the crazy ones. The misfits. The rebels. The troublemakers. The round pegs in the square holes. The ones who see things differently. They're not fond of rules. And they have no respect for the status quo. You can quote them, disagree with them, glorify or vilify them. About the only thing you can't do is ignore them. Because they change things. They push the human race forward. And while some may see them as the crazy ones, we see genius. Because the people who are crazy enough to think they can change the world, are the ones who do.

– Rob Siltanen, Creator, Apple 'Think Different' campaign

This book is dedicated to my grandchildren who will inherit our world and future.

Deja

Layla

Ela

CONTENTS

PROLOGUE

When you have eliminated the impossible, whatever remains, however improbable, must be the truth.

—Sir Arthur Conan Doyle

OFTEN IT IS NOT THAT WE FEAR NEW IDEAS AS MUCH AS we fear the truth. This is especially true when we examine ideas that are not indigenous to our culture. This examination can be truly terrifying. So, we opt for a condition of stasis by eliminating the possibility of there being more to know, rather than conceding to the fact that we might not know what lies beyond our ego. We are content, therefore, to man the battlements of our worldview and shut out any possibility that there may be more out there than we understand than we have ever perceived. This may be, in fact, the worst type of insidious ignorance.

I have come to understand that the human mind, together with the heart, has more than enough room to hold many types of knowledge and still be true to its most closely held concepts of what life means and the spiritual beliefs it holds dear. The caveat is that we must be able to free our minds so that it can soar and look, with kind eyes, on that which we do not understand. To be more specific, and bring the point of this book into focus, I speak here of our species' untiring quest to understand the meaning of life and the meaning of everything. This is, after all, a subject in which mankind has invested many millennia of effort to understand. The theme of this book is to conduct an honorable journey in search of truth, how we believe the truth, and what are the rules of truth.

Humanity does not lack variations of religious, philosophical, or metaphysical viewpoints. The world's greatest social structures are not bound by national or international borders, political ideas, ethnic ties, or even familial ties. The greatest single social structure resides in our general and global belief systems. To believe in a religious and spiritual viewpoint, in which something is greater than we are, is ubiquitous with being human. It is the most universal truth of all. Even more surprising is that when one performs a rudimentary examination of all the world's religious and spiritual life philosophies and viewpoints, we find more similarities than differences. Before civilization came into being, the anthropological record clearly shows that early humans (Homo neanderthalensis and Home sapiens) began to explore the deep secrets of self-existence. This was during the Middle Paleolithic period, about 300,000 years ago, with its end at the beginning of the Pleistocene period. Though there is some dispute among scholars, it appears that this was the first time that ceremonial burials were performed. It is also during this time that totemic practices began. Religious modernity followed a long line of cultural evolution dating back to about 50,000 years. Ever since humanity began, religiosity has edged along throughout all cultures, developing spiritual and religious belief systems, rules of conduct, and mutually accepted and commonly held laws of social and spiritual deportment within the vast social arena.

The pattern of this evolution repeats itself in a mix of virtually infinite details, time after time. All the time the theme coalesces around the idea that there must be some kind of super precedence (a being) greater than the individual. This phenomenon we call God (Christians), Yahweh (old Jewish Testament), Allah (Islam), Krishna (Hinduism), the Tao (Chinese), *Akal Purakh* (Sikhism), Ahura Mazda (Zoroastrianism), *Amaterasu* (Shinto Japan), and other countless names. All cultures have one God or constellation of gods and labels to put upon them. This word, God, is what we call this divine entity in the western world. But he, or she, or it, has had many names in different cultures at different times. When God appears in multiple forms, they are often one God, or a manifestation of the one God's characteristics or personalities, each of which specializes in some element of importance for its believers.

In some cases, the one God has universal and unlimited powers and complete purview over all things, while in other cases each manifestation specializes according to the beliefs of its adherents. This common theme is too similar to be coincidental. While there are many variations on this refrain, the human mind is not infinite in its imagination, and so we see that common patterns begin to emerge. The traits of the gods, or God, are innumerable but consistent among themselves. And logically so, because all human minds are consistent in forming underlying themes within their worldviews.

As far as we know, only humans have developed the concept of deities or forces; as far as we know, dogs and donkeys do not pray. I would suggest this can only be so because only humans are sentient. "Sentience is the capacity to feel, perceive, or experience subjectively." One could, therefore, be justified as an astral observer to inquire if humans invented God or it was the other way around. The verdict by the mass of human thinking (arrived at on their knees or perhaps in the lotus position) is in and so it seems God or the gods created everything based on the democratic doctrine the majority vote wins. This may or may not be the 'truth', but it is the way in which our collective human culture believes.

The question this book tries to answer is this: "Is the above the only possibility?"

Is a God or gods, who are themselves sentient, the only alternative to the question of who we are and why we exist? How much more can we discover?

To attempt to do this, we must address the issue of truth. What is the truth? How can we know it? How can we verify it? What is the evidence and how can we possibly challenge the collective will of billions of human beings throughout history? The answer is at once obvious. A majority viewpoint is not necessarily the truth. At one time, the greatest European minds believed that the world was flat and that we were surrounded by an undetectable ether. History and Enlightenment ushered in the facts and proved these ideas to be false. In the writing of this book, the subject of "truth" is once again locked in a bitter dispute. It seems that truth has now been relegated to the area of opinion. It is squabbled over like pieces of meat among a pack of dogs, torn in one way, and then another. This is not the trait of an enlightened, gentle, and rational mind.

TRUTH

A truth that's told with bad intent beats all the lies you can invent.

—William Blake

TRUTH IS NOT ARBITRARY AND IS ALWAYS SUPPORTED by rigorous and reliable evidence. Truth must match facts and reality. Further, it must have fidelity to a standard acceptable by all persons of good faith and scrupulous judgment. Over time, the concept of truth has become a subject of discourse among traditional, legal, philosophical, scientific, and religious/spiritual stakeholders, and theories, about what makes up truth have been established by accepted modes of judgment. This scholarly discourse gives credence and an intellectual foundation to what is it that we can rely upon.

Martin Heidegger (1889–1976), the German philosopher, held that the original meaning of truth, according to the ancient Greeks, was an essence of "un-concealment." The original concept of truth was called *Alethia*. Eventually, this became known as *veritas* by the Greeks.

The stakeholders have continued to debate how to identify truth from falsehood. Humans use language to communicate, so the meaning of what we say using the words we speak or write or, in some cases, communication is expressed through symbols (as in mathematics), so it must be included in an analysis of the augments concerning truth. These boundaries are called the "criterion of truth." This further leads to the question of the role that faith-based and empirical knowledge play. These roles will further be examined in this chapter. Deciding how words, beliefs, and symbols can be considered "true" is the focus of the five substantive theories we will now examine. These theories are rooted in the widely accepted and shared view of published scholars. We must recognize the categories that will be studied further. The first category to examine is the substantive theories. They are not universally accepted. The second category includes the deflationary theories which have been developed more recently. We will consider the deflationary theory as well in this chapter.

Let us look at the definition of substantive theory as laid down by Avinash Dixit in *Lawlessness and Economics* (2004, 22):

"The aim of a substantive theory should be to construct a collection of models that is sufficiently small but memorable enough to use and still cover an optimally large portion of the spectrum of facts."

The substantive theories thus represent a collection of truth that covers the widest range of related theories and facts.

The first of the theories is the correspondence theory. The simplest way to understand this theory is to understand that it is proposed to be true and corresponds to the facts. This was the position that was taken by Socrates, Plato, and Aristotle. The principle behind this idea is that something true or false is always related to a "suchness." This suchness holds the fidelity of the thing that is being taken as true or false. The philosopher/theologian, Thomas Aquinas, stated the idea as follows: "A judgment is said to be true when it conforms to external reality." There are some problems with this theory because some languages do not provide a clear translation regarding the essential nature of "truth." Alfred Tarski's semantic theory deals with this issue, and we will discuss it later in the book.

The next theory, coherence, states that it is essential that the element of a truth. "A coherence theory of truth states that the truth of any (true) proposition consists in its coherence with some specified set of propositions." (Stanford Encyclopedia of Philosophy 1996)

Elements of the argument for truth must mutually reinforce each other. If, for example, a person asserts that she/he was an eyewitness to an event but was found to be at a distant location at the time they claim to have witnessed the event, there is a lack of coherence. Therefore, being a witness to the event is not supported by coherence. The facts do not support the assertion. Nonetheless, other scholars on the subject reject coherence theory as, in general, lacking justification in its application to other areas of truth. The counterview revolves around specific areas of inquiry concerning the natural world. Empirical data, in general, asserts practical matters of psychology and society with the support of other major theories of truth.

The next theory, constructivist theory, was championed by such philosophical luminaries as Spinoza, Leibniz, G.W.F. Hegel, and F.H. Bradley. Constructivist theory is more accurately labeled social constructivism because it asserts that truth is reflected by struggles within the community, it is culture-specific. It views the perception of truth as dependent on many elements such as human perception and social experience. Truth, therefore, is viewed as a construction of the perceived realities of the individual or community, regarding specific situations. In it, there is a strong tie to physical and biological realities like race, gender, etc.

G. Vico, a philosopher, stated, "that history and culture were man-made." Thus, this theory has an epistemological view concerning truth. In this theory, truth is said to be profoundly influenced by human culture and its components, as noted above, such as race and gender.

Consensus theory, in its simplest form, holds that whatever is agreed upon is the truth. In some iteration of this theory, the truth must be agreed upon by some group. A proponent of this theory was J. Habermas (Jürgen Habermas currently ranks as one of the most influential philosophers in the world, but it was countered by Karl Marx, *in A Contribution to the Critique of Political Economy (1859),* [2] who is more closely aligned with conflict theory in relation to society and its motivations. It is noted that in the Islamic Koran, Muhammad stated that "My community can never agree upon an error." This can be loosely compared to the Catholic belief that the Pope can never err in matters of faith and morals. The American jury system seems to rely on this principle as well; however, we know the jury system can be flawed and there have been results of some defendants being judged guilty and then later being exonerated when circumstance showed that they were, in fact, innocent.

The pragmatic theory is somewhat faceted and there are three schools of thought on the subject. It was introduced in the twentieth century by C.S. Pierce, W. James, and J. Dewey. They did not completely agree on the details, but generally believed that truth could only be verified by putting the results of "agreed truth" into practice. The crux of Peirce's pragmatism is that for any statement to be meaningful, it must have practical bearings. Peirce saw the pragmatic account of meaning as a method for clearing up metaphysics and aiding scientific inquiry.. (Peirce 1931–58).

William James, on the other hand, held that the theory was more complex. He felt that truth was a quality. Its value could only be confirmed by its effectiveness when the concept is applied to practice. In other words, if something is purported to be true, and when the underlying issue is tested and found to be accurate, only then we can say that the issue is actually true. John Dewey's subtle variation was that an inquiry into some element of truth could be judged true, only if "openly submitted" to the test by a community of appropriate and knowledgeable judges and if it passed the test. It is clear that pragmatic theory is nuanced and somewhat shadowy in construction, but all views correspond to the practical results of something said to be true. The famous theoretical physicist Richard Feynman somewhat fatalistically said of the pragmatic theory that "we could never know with certainty if something were true. We could only know with certainty if it were false."

Minimalist (deflationary) theory (not a substantiated theory) is a relatively new theory, a second bite of the apple if you will. In short, it says that just because something is old, does not necessarily mean that it is correct. This theory relies on the use of predicates (as in the truth of the matter is predicated in $2 + 2 = 4$). Pundits claim that predicates are not normally used in common language. So, in ordinary language we may say that "snow is white" but, in fact, there might be dirty snow which is not white but gray or brown. This renders the statement a kind of paradox until we investigate the matter more thoroughly. It is said by deflationary theorists that the word "true" is just semantic convenience. Personally, I find this line of reasoning tedious, but that is just me.

There are a few other theories in the category of truth, but I am going to move on into areas less esoteric and a little more commonly understood. Formal theories are as follows:

Logical Truth

Logic is concerned with the rigid patterns or steps in reason that help distinguish if an assertion is true or false. I will provide a concrete example of this when we discuss Meno later. A logical truth is determined by the analysis of facts agreed upon by the participant(s) of the argument. The constituent elements of the argument are taken to be empirical and undisputed by consensus of the one(s) analyzing the proposition. So, let us say that the argument is $4 + 4 = 8$. We all agree that this is a true mathematical statement because the elements of the equation are conceded to have values which are true in themselves.

Mathematical truth is a bit more complicated because mathematics is constrained in being a formal language with specific rules. Though typically, an average person may consider mathematics to be straightforward, the professional may consider it quite the opposite. Mathematics has its limitations. Specific examples of this lie in Kurt Friedrich Gödel's incompleteness theorems. Church–Turing thesis also contributed to the limitations of mathematics in the early part of the twentieth century. If the reader is interested, they can explore these theories further in books that expand on the subject. The details of these are not essential to this discussion, but it suffices to say that mathematics at higher levels does have limitations. However, for the layman, mathematics is reliable.

The Semantic Theories of Truth

This is one of my favorite areas of truth. It is the one where a layperson can prove or disprove truth based on the words they use, and the meaning attached to them. We must understand that no universal language exists and, therefore, complete translation for every concept can't be accomplished for every language. Thus, the semantic theory is language-specific. We owe this train of thought to Alfred Tarski, who was a mathematician, a logician, and a philosopher. Tarski was responsible for the development of mathematical truth in semantic theory. For example, strictly speaking, there is no word for "goodbye" in Spanish. Spanish speakers do have words that have a feeling that conveys a parting, that is, *adios,* (go with God is implied) with God.

Historical and Cultural Truth Theory

Across all cultures throughout history, humankind has struggled with the concept of truth. The Greeks studied it in detail as far back as pre-Socratic time (610 BCE) and have a long history with the subject and have contributed the fundamental tenets of truth to the Western culture. In Hinduism, the truth has come to be defined as "unchangeable." Today modern India's national motto is *Satyameva Jayvate* (Truth alone wins). Historically, the Upanishads, dating back to the 7th–6th centuries BCE, and written in Sanskrit, are among the earliest known writing concerning the Hindu view of truth. According to Islamic philosophy, also known as Avicenna, what corresponds in the mind to what is outside it, is truth. This is one view that is expanded upon by the following phrase: "Truth is also said of the veridical belief in the existence (of something)." In the Middle Ages, Aquinas makes the statement that "Truth is the conformity between the intellect and the thing."

In Religion: Omniscience or Awareness

Some worldviews, in a religious context concerning truth, reside within the purview of a divine being. These would include some but not all Buddhist and Abrahamic belief systems, Christianity, Islam, and Judaism. This truth is based on faith and cultural–religious/spiritual customs. Most, but not all (not religious/spiritualism), of the information presented so far is "practical and is based on intellectualism." It is commonly accepted that determining the truth is not for the faint-hearted. It can often be difficult and mind-bending work. It can be torturous and excruciatingly difficult to untie the knot of falsehood. The words used in dispensing information, that is ultimately untrue, maybe cloaked in layers of inaccuracy, with each layer subtler than the ones that precede it. The proponent(s) of untrue information will try to beguile us with outright lies or false logic that prods our minds into submission. Untruth can be like the song of the fabled mermaid that beckons sailors to their doom on the shoals (of deceit); deceit that is designed to be beautiful.

We should be aware that truth, in religious teachings, is based on faith and not fact. Believers may disagree, but such beliefs never seem to be able to pass the test for truth presented in the aforementioned categories of truth.

So, if the task is to distill truth from falsehood, how are we to proceed? As a standard practice in this book, I suggest that we look at the beginning, for an anchor point, from which to launch our quest. It is important to note that we will circle back to the kinds of truth that we have already stated before. For now, we shall begin with philosophy.

The study of truth is a property that most firmly lies within the realm of philosophy. Nearly 98 percent of Western intellectual progress and knowledge (for the past 2500 years and longer for Eastern spiritualism) can be attributed to philosophy. The study of philosophy is the study of the fundamental nature of knowledge, reality, and existence. But philosophy is a strange bird. It is neither art nor science in the strictest terms, and many misinformed pundits of this subject proclaim that philosophy cannot prove anything empirically. Allow me to provide an example to the contrary using deductive logic, a branch of philosophy:

If A = B and B is greater than C, then A is greater than C.

It is true that in today's world of the hard sciences, philosophy is considered, by some, to be too ethereal and unbound, which is reflected in its shorthand title **PhD** often sarcastically translated into "piled higher and deeper." Those who opt for this, only expose their lack of education or worse a fear of accepting what they do not understand.

The point is made by the skeptic who argues "what can we really know?"

The French philosopher, René Descartes (1596–1650) addressed the quandary of "what we can really know" in his famous pronouncement "I think therefore I am" (Latin: *Cogito ergo sum*). Further, he provided a dialogue on the subject, which is quoted below:

But I have convinced myself that there is absolutely nothing in the world, no sky, no earth, no minds, and no bodies. Does it now follow that I, too, do not exist? No. If I convinced myself of something or thought anything at all, then I certainly existed. But there is a deceiver of supreme power and cunning who deliberately and constantly deceives me. In that case, I, too, undoubtedly exist, if he deceives me, and let him deceive me as much as he can, he will never bring it about that I am nothing, so long as I think that I am something. So, after considering everything very thoroughly, I must finally conclude that the proposition, I am, I exist, is necessarily true whenever it is put forward by me or conceived in my mind.

—(AT VII 25; CSM II 16-17)

The great philosophers of the past have also considered this argument. What Descartes realized is that he knows, he exists, just by experiencing "being." As the experiencer, he also knows that anything conceived (as being true) by his mind, by extension also exists.

It is philosophy that rescues us from this existential quandary. It cannot be stressed too vigorously why philosophical thinking must be the foundation of our quest for truth, it is as legitimate as any science. It is also like science in that it is ever-evolving as new, and allows for more productive ideas to enlighten our worldview. In this process, new and more accurate ideas replace outdated ones. Philosophical tenets were never intended to be monolithic. Like science, philosophy is a growing, living thing.

Before we go on, let us look at another philosophical example of what is called "absolute truth," this time with the use of geometry. In the following example, Meno is an associate of Socrates. The dialogue was later written down by Plato. In the dialogue, Socrates engages Meno in a discussion concerning, what he calls, "true virtue." This, in turn, leads to a discussion on "real knowledge." To illustrate his point, Socrates asks Meno if he can use the assistance of one of Meno's slaves, a young boy. Meno agrees and Socrates begins asking the boy a series of questions. Socrates does not "lead" the boy to the answers that he wants, but rather frames his questions carefully and "walks" the boy through a series of steps in a logical manner so that the boy can come to his own conclusion. First, Socrates draws a square on a piece of parchment and asks the boy what he sees. Then he draws three more identical squares so that all four are adjacent to each other and form a larger square. He asks the boy what he sees, and the boy acknowledges that he now sees four squares combined to form a picture that creates one larger square. Socrates draws a diagonal line inside the first square, starting at the lower left-hand corner and finishing at the upper right-hand corner. He then asks the boy what he sees now. The boy describes that the first box has been divided to form two right-angled triangles which are exactly half the size of the square. Socrates now draws a similar diagonal line through each of the remaining squares.

For clarity, I have drawn the squares as described, and have colored and labeled them as Boxes 1, 2, 3, and 4. The red line captures the four squares (boxes) and shows how they delineate a larger square. Then I added the diagonal lines that bisect each of the four small squares. I add a yellow line that delineates a smaller square. I colored one of the right-angled triangles to show that it forms a shape that is exactly half of the area of the first square. This square, I have labeled Box 1. See the illustration below.

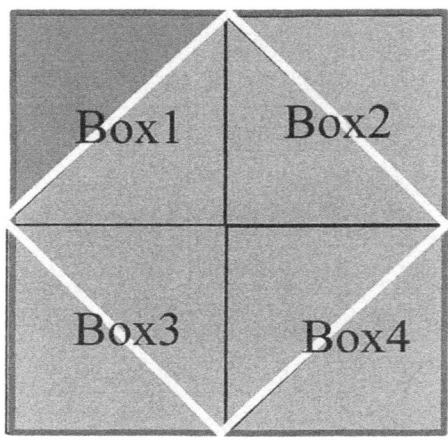

Socrates now asks the boy what is the size relation of the larger square (red) to the newly formed smaller square (yellow). The boy realized that the triangle in the original square equals one half of its area, which can only mean that each triangle that forms the second square (yellow) must equal one-quarter of the area of the (yellow) smaller square. And so, the smaller (yellow) square must equal one half of the larger (red) square. This is Socrates's proof of truth through the use of geometry. It forms a mathematical certainty that is self-evident.

The point of this exercise is to illustrate that philosophy is grounded in the real world. Of course, there are other realms within the study of various philosophical areas that do not lend themselves to such clear-cut results. These areas, however, have been rigorously explored by other philosophers to this day. Philosophers specifically want to know what sort of things are "true and what sort of things are "false," if the principal issue is "what is true." We have already looked at the major truth theories above. For now, let us concentrate on the essence of philosophy, and why this is the tool we have used to understand the truth.

PHILOSOPHY

Truth in philosophy means that concept and external reality correspond.

—Georg W.F. Hegel (1770–1831)

ARISTOTLE ONCE SAID, "ALL MEN BY NATURE DESIRE knowledge." The more I consider his words, the more important I believe this chapter is. If it is any indication of how seriously correct, I believe, Aristotle's remark is. I must admit to you that this is the fourth rewrite of the chapter; I must get this right. The chapter contains an abbreviated yet broad historical account of the technicalities regarding philosophy. My trepidation is that the readers will become bogged down by repetitive names, dates, and other details, and find themselves overwhelmed by academic minutiae. Though this book, and the current chapter, is not about entertaining the reader, I do hope you are entertained in the same way in which we all are when we indulge in the act of gazing into the night sky, with no thought other than to contemplate the majesty of the heavens. You might find the reading enlightening and entertaining if you have not had time to explore your mental and spiritual interests. That is, if you are a curious person who enjoys ideas and concepts. It is not esoteric but rather more like a common snowflake, intricate and beautiful.

From the very outset, let me clarify that the study of philosophy has its share of ardent detractors which, by the way, offer no better alternative than a quick detour to "common sense." The common sense to which they refer, in this context, is a code for a supposed agreement about some assertion that may or may not be true. This kind of common sense is most often not accurate and is generally not subjected to rigorous proof. It is often a red herring thrown out as a sophist claim which, loosely translated, means "well, everybody knows …." It is proclaimed without the slightest authority. The alternative legitimate common sense, which also exists, is distinguished as simply describing what we know based on individual or collective experience. This sort of common sense has a history behind it. So, it is common sense that a lame horse runs slowly. We may believe that this is common sense without a protracted debate. If we are to complete this journey successfully, we must start on very solid ground. I have proposed philosophy (the love of knowledge) as our foundation. From the outset, we should ask what authority do we turn to in order to distinguish true knowledge? Further, knowledge of what? Which human endeavor (study) are we to employ to understand how to arrive at true knowledge?

This is a field that stands apart from religion, art, science, spirituality, and metaphysics, and yet it encompasses elements of all of them. Philosophy literally translated from *Philosophia*, the original

Greek word meaning "love of wisdom." It studies the general and fundamental issues concerning matters of knowledge, values, reason, existence, language, and the mind. It plunges deep into the cryptic questions of existentialism such as the following: Is it possible to really know anything? Do humans really have free will? What is the nature of truth(?) There are many more such questions. To gain an accurate understanding of the topic, we are required to wade through a tangle of phrases that relate to concepts inside our minds with which we struggle for clarity. The clarity in understanding these concepts is of the utmost importance. Description of ideas, spoken or written, must be clear. We are empirically climbing the steps of knowledge, and each step is only useful if the preceding steps are rendered unambiguous.

The study of philosophy is a grand journey, not because it is difficult (which it sometimes is) but because of its grandness in width and depth. Width in the sense that it is at the root of human intellectual and spiritual thought. It covers an enormous range of subordinate fields or areas such as the sciences, theology, metaphysics, the arts, thought, epistemology, ethics, aesthetics, logic, history, languages, and politics, objectivity, and subjectively to mention a few. It is deep because it penetrates their very roots. We will explore each topic, as the best minds of history have thought, to discuss them, contemplate over them, and endeavored to explain them.

We study philosophy in all its major forms because it is the foundation of wisdom and knowledge. This then is our point of departure and will build up from here.I ask for your patience as I try to give a brief description, in a manner that is both enjoyable and thorough. I will try to keep the explanations of concepts and meanings as short as possible.

From the outset, we must agree on how we can know the truth. For 2500 years, humankind has engaged it's brightest and most learned minds to the task of deciphering this quandary. Any other starting point is just opinion, not the truth.

After we consider the scholarly elements of philosophy, we will explore the practical tools that it provides us with in our daily lives. The study of philosophy is traditionally divided into three major branches:

- Moral philosophy called "ethos" or ethics.
- Natural philosophy which includes physics, mathematics, logic, etc.
- Metaphysics which includes esoteric realms of existence, causation, God, etc.

We shall see that the three branches can be further broken down into sub-categories. But first, let us review its historical and geographical aspects.

In the United States, we are most familiar with the Western view of philosophy and trace it back to the Greek thinkers. Thales (c.624–546 BC) and Pythagoras (c.570–495 BC) practiced what was call *Philosophia*, other notable scholars within this group include Socrates, Plato, and Aristotle. Many others have come to represent "the ancient Greco-Roman" school. Some Roman philosophers included Cicero and Seneca. It was this collection of early Western philosophers who laid down the foundations for the study of knowledge and set the bedrock which we follow today.

The medieval period (fifth to fifteenth century) was punctuated by the fall of the Roman empire, and the emergence of Christianity under the Roman emperor Constantine. It is no surprise that we see the movement of philosophical concerns turn toward Judeo-Christian theology. Innovative viewpoint began to focus on theological themes such as the existence and nature of God, the nature of faith, and the place of reason. Key philosophical minds such as St. Thomas Aquinas, St. Augustine, Boethius, and Rodger Bacon assured that philosophy harmonized well with theology and the interpretation of Holy scripture. We see some overlap of the medieval period with the Renaissance (1355–1650) when a new focus on classic Greco-Roman thought comes into being. This was followed by early modern philosophy. This school moved away from religious to secular, and then into the so-called rational thought. The rise of Thomas Hobbes and René Descartes ushered in the era of the natural sciences. At its core, it was a rational foundation for knowledge.

During the Enlightenment period, the likes of Locke, Spinoza, Leibniz, Hume, and Kant populated the pantheon of scholars. In the twentieth century, we see the emergence of a split in the schools of thought into analytic philosophy and continental philosophy. Other movements included existentialism, logical pragmatism, and others.

In the Near East, "wisdom literature" is the name that has been given to the philosophies of the Fertile Crescent of Iran and Arabia.

Today, this area of study is mostly interpreted as a part of the Islamic culture. Its aim was to educate its adherents in ethical action, practical living, and virtue. This was accomplished by traditional stories and proverbs.

In the ancient history of Egypt, a text known as *Sebayt* was incorporated into the lives of the faithful. Egyptian philosophy is closely related to guiding its people through religion and law.

Geonim, from the Talmudic Academies in Babylon, influenced the inhabitants of the area. Maimonides, one of the most renowned Torah scholars, was known to engage the Greeks with Islamic and Jewish philosophy. The pre-Islamic Iranian philosophy begins with Zoroaster who was one of the first to promote monotheism and the dualism between good and evil.

It was the culture of India that gave us Gautama Buddha between the sixth and fourth centuries BCE. Buddhism eventually spread to Tibet, China, and the entire Far East. Today, it is a worldwide spiritual philosophy. Buddhist doctrine is concerned with the true nature of a thing and our ignorance of them. Key concepts include anatta (non-self) and anicca (the transience of all things). This study is not intended to denigrate the contribution of the Indian Mahabharata, the Upanishads, or the Vedas for these form the backbone of ancient Indian philosophy (fourth century BCE).

Chinese philosophy is old and dates approximately from the sixth century to 221 BCE. The schools of Confucianism, legalism, and Daoism dominated this period. Included in the traditions which spouted during this time were metaphysical, political, and ethical theories that embodied ideas such as Toa, yin-yang, ren, and lin. As you can see, China has had a long history of philosophical thought and tradition.

African philosophy is a product of its rampant fractionalization. There is no practical method for us to know all African philosophical concepts, across all the African continent, and at all times. This vast area is characterized by small tribes (in some cases these tribes coalesced into large tribal nations) each with their histories and philosophical ideas. It was not until the seventeenth century that Ethiopian philosophy developed a thriving, strong identity of its own. The luminaries included Zera Yacob and Anton Wilhelm Amo.

Native American philosophies can be characterized in much the same way as the African model. The large collection of tribes across the North American continent makes it difficult to delve deeply into the multiple variations of cultures. The worship of ancestor and Earth element (animal, the sky, rivers, mountains, the wind, and the seasons) are known to be common. Living with nature, and in harmony, characterizes (in a very generalized way) the culture of North American tribal populations. Mesoamerican, Aztec in Central America, and Inca in South America can be said to dominate a discourse of these populations. Aztec philosophy was an intellectual tradition. It was developed by Tlamatini (people who know). These practices and ideas were kept in codices. Aztecs believed in universal energy known as *Ometeotl*. It promoted the concept of balance in day-to-day living and dealing with a constantly changing world. The Aztec spiritual worldview was said to have strong elements of pantheism embedded within it. *Tlamatiliztli* (wisdom) centered on a balanced (middle) way of living.

Amawtakuna were the elite philosophers and scholars of the Incas. They were the teachers of religion, tradition, history, and ethics. They believed in the theory of "complementary opposites." This is similar to the concept seen in the Chinese philosophy of yin and yang. These complementary aspects such as up and down, man and woman, dark and light are seen as a harmonious whole. Today, we can see "complementarian elements" in modern quantum physics (QP).

The whole of human philosophy, and the amount of time for which the discipline has been practiced, is far beyond the scope of this book. But, by now you can see the common threads that are woven throughout the fabric of this very human endeavor. The details vary between cultures, and over time, but the essential themes remain generally intact. In all these cases, humans have strived to understand themselves and the physical and spiritual world in which they live. So, it seems that the search for how the world appears and its relation to what is true is firmly embedded in the many practices of the philosophies that humans have adopted throughout time, and across the many cultures. "What is truth," is a question that our species has asked from the very beginning. Humanity has codified and studied the many elements and foundations that have been essential to defining us and our search for methods to discern truthfulness from falsehood and reality from imagination. We have, as a species, invested millennia of effort and scholarship seeking wisdom to help build our way. Before we leave this investigative journey into the history and geography of philosophy, let us take one last look at the various categories that focus philosophical study into discreet concepts.

The categories were created as a logical way for scholars and students to discuss a broad range of philosophical subjects, and then divide them into smaller, digestible, sub-groupings to focus their study on specific topics.

Metaphysics is the study of certain features of reality. Some of these features are ethereal, while others are more solid. General features include the concept of existence, time, causation, and the relationship between mind and body. Metaphysics also includes cosmology, ontology, and the study of being. It looks at thorny issues such as the relationship between what is perceived and what "is."

Epistemology is the study of knowledge. It considers the source of knowledge and where knowledge comes from? What in intuition, a priori reason, memory, perception, testimony, and self-knowledge? Key among its questions, and the one significant for our current investigation, is "What is truth?" Epistemologists even ask whether "true knowledge is possible." There is an area of study in epistemology that considers religion and explores concepts like the soul, afterlife, religious experience, God, the relationship between science and religion, religious vocabulary, and religious texts.

Value theory considers subjects such as beauty, goodness, and justice. It articulates arguments concerning political views and values, feminist issues, and the law in general.

Ethics enquires into morals, good and bad conduct, political philosophy, the law, and much more. Its main branches are non-native ethics, meta-ethics, and applied ethics.

Aesthetics reviews how we perceive beauty, culture, and nature. It enquires into subjects such as tastes, emotional values, and enjoyment. Aesthetics can be viewed as being concerned with sensory and emotional ideals.

The study of government and its relationship between the individual, all levels of social interaction such as the clan, family, communities, and the state, and the considerations of the obligations between and among these interactions is called pollical philosophy.

Logic is the realm of reasoning and argument. Logic can be understood as a chain of connected premises that lead to a premise. We saw such an example in Socrates' Meno.

Science is a discipline based on a reasoned foundation of propositions, the structure of formations in thought, tests, and the implications that result from it. The basic tool of science is the scientific method, which is as follows: Formulate a question, create a hypothesis or conjecture, form a prediction based on the conjecture, test the prediction through experimentation, analyze the results that prove or falsify the prediction. The results are called a theory and are only help to be true when another theory "cannot" replace it.

At last, we come to the consideration of the practical application of philosophy. This is called applied philosophy. This is described as our innate ability, as humans, to absorb from, wherever we can, whatever life experience illuminates our consciousness. Our teachers are our parents and extended families, our faith in what we believe spiritually or religiously, our education system, mentors that show up on the doorstep of our life, and our ability to weave all this into the fabric of a cohesive system of values. We are all autodidactic (self-taught) and one way or another we absorb the wisdom that comes from just living day-to-day life. We will assimilate all the lessons of all our experiences, formal and informal, to form our personal philosophy of life.

There are pitfalls along the way and many of us stray from what is true and move instead toward what we espouse to be true. The two may often come in conflict with each other. This is because of the "ego." We often don't desire the truth when it does not support our agendas. I believe that no one can lie more convincingly to us than ourselves. So, there is no hope for the truth when there is no solid philosophical framework to support our ideas. A person in such a state will not be able to find the truth. As the Zen saying goes, "it is the person who rides the back of an ox who looks the world over for an ox."

Applied philosophy is not an abstraction. It is the putting into action of the wisdom from two-and-a-half centuries of the teaching, in all (applicable areas) of mankind, the noblest thought. We have covered but a fraction of the entirety of what philosophy is and what it teaches. Thousands of books, codices, manuals, and traditions are devoted to this subject and its myriad sub-divisions. But they all have one thing in common, to seek the truth, to give us a foundation for judging and informing ourselves of what we can rely upon.

To study truth through philosophy and come to sagacious conclusions which can be relied upon, is the aim of the study of truth through the study of philosophy. In certain matters, opinion is enough, but we must remember that not everyone shares the same opinions and, in most cases, that is perfectly acceptable. But, in other areas, opinion will never do. There are situations in which truth matters. In these cases, sometimes life and death hang in the balance. Raw belief can lead to disastrous states pitting one person against another, or even a whole nation against another. This is why wars are fought, injustice, bigotry, and intolerance created, and enmity unleashed on all those involved. Opinion, when carried to an extreme, can be as corrosive as any acid.

We need solid ground, a logical framework of laws, a system that guides us and gives humanity cohesive standards for conduct, and therefore the study of philosophy and its search for truth is vital.

EVIDENCE

Tell people that there is an invisible man, in the sky who created the universe, and the vast majority will believe you. Tell them the paint is wet, and they have to touch it to be sure.

—George Carlin

EVIDENCE IS FUNDAMENTAL TO SUPPORTING AND PROVING a statement or proposition. Yet, these days, we seem to require such little evidence before we accept something as the truth. Perhaps this is so because we live in a time when most of us have abdicated our trust in our collective social and intellectual group. These are times when our associates, friends, and colleagues become smaller, not so much in quantity, but in the diversity of worldviews. So, for instance, if we are politically liberal most, if not all, of the people in our immediate orbit of influence or who add credence to our views, will be cut from the same cloth. This is true for the moderates and conservatives as well. By taking our talking points from such biased sources such as radio, TV, texts, the Internet, friends, and associates, we only reinforce the ideas which support our choice of what we call the truth. This inevitably leads to circular biased worldviews, with us hardly noticing what is happening.

I recently asked a conservative friend of mine what he thought of the current proposal by the Republican senate's debate on its Health Care bill, in consideration of the dire predictions made by the House Budget Committee (CBO). The committee has proposed that tens of millions of people would be left without medical insurance if the proposed legislation is passed as it is. He replied with the popular conservative refrain that the CBO often gets the numbers wrong, and so we should not pay much attention to it. I was curious, so I consulted respectable, nonpartisan, fact-checking Internet sites on his assertion. They collectively showed that this assertion was misleading. The difference in the CBO's projections for the previous administration's healthcare plan was only 0.07 percent of what the CBO had actually projected. Well, I thought, I should call my friend a gloat. No, that initial idea would be incorrect because, as usual, one statistic would not tell the whole story. So, I continued to research further and what I found was enlightening. That original statistic was accurate but, it still turns out that the CBO is often off its mark. I dug further to find the reason. It's because the types of predictions the CBO makes are excruciatingly difficult to predict exactly in the best of times. The simple reason for this is that there are too many variables, and the time involved maybe decades.

How would I reply to my friend now? I rethought the question and decided it needed to be reframed to accurately express my real concern. What I wanted to know was how he felt about the CBO's prediction that millions of Americans would lose their medical insurance. The CBO projecting about 23,000,000. The real question should have been how he felt about CBO's projection for a loss of coverage for tens of thousands of American citizens. If his answer was the same, I could have probed further and conceded, "yes it could be wrong, but how many Americans losing health insurance was acceptable to him." For the sake of argument, let's say half the estimated number, that would be 11,500,000. To those who would lose their insurance, and I suspect most Americans, the answer is that the number is unacceptable. The fact of the matter, in this case, is that the CBO is only a reasonable barometer of the effects that the health-care legislation will have on the predicted number of Americans. The fact that the CBO exists at all is testimony that the government needs to have reasonable evidence for the projected results of its actions. Otherwise, it would have no guide at all.

This is how evidence works. We hope it will be accurate enough, have a strong vitality of its own, and be considered in a broad enough view to be convincing. We need to understand that human contrivances can never be a 100 percent perfect, a 100 percent of the time, but they can be more than enough.

When I started this chapter regarding what is acceptable evidence, I did not know exactly where it might lead me. But because of this example, I know that now it is more involved than I thought. I checked the federal record regarding its rule for admissible evidence in a court proceeding. There are over one thousand line-items pertaining to the aspects of what does and does not qualify as acceptable evidence.

I looked deeper and consulted philosophical works that elucidated the subject. There is quite a bit of reliable data on the question. The first bit of information was the most useful. The classic definition of evidence is this: "Evidence is that which justifies belief."

The problem, however, as far as philosophy is concerned, is that beyond this point, the path leads down a slippery slope. Several philosophical possibilities can arise. For example, we could turn to the philosophical arguments concerning what is knowable or other existential issues.

Other examples of how evidence is affected are common. For example, counterexamples of competing for an idea for evidence exists. In these situations, a counter and competing line of reasoning can dilute the veracity of the original evidence.

A classic example is the theory of creationism. Creationism is defined as "the belief that the universe and living organisms originate from specific acts of divine creator," as in the Biblical account, rather than by natural processes such as evolution. Creationists proclaim that many living creatures seem perfectly suited for the environments they inhabit, and therefore they must have been designed by God to align themselves to the environment precisely. But Darwinism provides a scientific rationale model, which more closely fits what we observe in the real world by way of the sciences of geology, paleontology, biology, genetics, and history, and explains the situation in a cogent and satisfying way without having to rely on a God whose existence cannot be proven by substantiated scientific fact. No matter how worthy the belief in God is, the belief in God is based on faith not on validated evidence. I understand some will take umbrage with this, so, for now, I will address it in another chapter.

Even if this was untrue, the very existence of counterexamples dilutes the evidence of the creationists to a point where it cannot be a 100 percent reliable.

In this case, we also note that belief is the antithesis of proof. David Hume, in *An Inquiry Concerning Understanding,* said, "A wise man proportions his belief to the evidence."

According to an article by the Stanford Encyclopedia of Philosophy, The International Cognition & Culture Institute (ICCI), "David Hume, born May 7, 1711":

As a general matter, the evidence seems to play a mediating role vis-à-vis or effort to arrive at an accurate picture of the world; we seek to believe what is true by means of holding beliefs that are well-supported by the evidence and seek to avoid believing what is false by mean of not holding beliefs that are not well-supported by the evidence.

Blanchard summarizes the picture well: "Surely the only possible rule, one may say, is to believe what is true and disbelieve what is false."

And, of course, that would be the rule if we were always in a position to know what was true and what was false. The whole difficulty arises from the fact we do not and often cannot know this. What is to guide us? "The idea is to believe no more, but also no less, than what the evidence warrants" (Stanford Encyclopedia of Philosophy 1974, 410–411).

Another important issue is all the discourse of evidence that comes into play when we arrive at the subject of the "burden of proof." Who is responsible to provide the proof through evidence? This task is held to be the responsibility of that person or body that makes an assertion and is asking others to believe the assertion. In modern times, this is an important point and it should be noted that the "party to be convinced" does not have the obligation to prove otherwise. However, this is not the same as not having the responsibility to rebut the asserter's evidence and proof.

We do have to ask what degree of certitude must be supported. This depends. It depends on what is being asserted. In the case of criminal law, it is usually a point "beyond a reasonable doubt." Generally, this level of certainty can be accepted in most cases, but it may also depend on the nature and subject of what is being asserted. In these cases, we focus on the evidence and examine both its quantity and quality. Some situations are cut and dry according to the proponents of the argument and are specific to the worldview it advocates. Religion is one of those areas of difficulty. I will not delve too deep into this because it will be covered more deeply in another chapter, but it is sufficient to say that there is a big difference between demonstrable fact and the ability to provide it.

The case for scientific evidence, and the resulting theorem, is a function of the scientific method. The first course of action is to provide a hypothesis which one believes to be true, then to test the possible outcomes. Once a theory is formed (based on the rules of scientific theory building), the outcomes are submitted for peer review and the proponent(s) must defend the theory again all challenges.

Jurisprudence, which is the theory and philosophy of law, takes a very structured approach to evidence. This method uses what is called the "rules of evidence." It is the foundation for law, and without it, the whole edifice of the legal system would fall into chaos. Certain kinds of evidence are prohibited from being used, for example, hearsay, anecdotal, or circumstantial. These lack the absolute vitality to prove (beyond the shadow of a doubt) that the evidence is strong and reliable enough to be considered viable evidence. It is not enough to say a friend of a friend said so-and-so, or given the circumstances, X must be true.

Using eyewitness testimony has been a practice from ancient times to modern times. But, at present, as a modern society, we have come to realize that eyewitness testimony is often flawed and not considered to be a 100 percent reliable.

Throughout much of the history of humanity various forms of torture have been utilized. It has been generally deemed ineffective because the person being tortured will confess to anything simply to stop the physical and mental pain of torture. This practice go hand-in-hand with self-confession or one elicited through various levels of cohesion.

During human history, practices like saliva tests have been used where the presumed guilty had a hot iron touch to their tongues. The guilty were presumed to have dry tongues, while the innocent wet. So, the wet tongue would protect the innocent.

Written evidence has been around for about 5000 years. This has been used successfully, and at other times, because of technology, less so.

More recently, the discovery and validation of evidence have been subject to scientific inquiry such as skin cell, hair, fingerprints, DNA, material testing, video, and electronic testing.

How does the study of evidence fit in with the premise of this book? In the prologue of this book, I put the question of how we might explore the furthest limits of our understanding of what the meaning of life is. The reason for the foregoing chapters was to set the stage for this inquiry. It is my view that without having a foundation from which to proceed with the solid ground underfoot, we wouldn't have a place to begin. Therefore, we looked at the study of knowledge through philosophy, the foundation of all knowledge—truth, its structure and theory, and, finally, evidence to support the proposition taken to be true. It is my opinion that without a foundation for our search, we would wander endlessly through time, ideology, and speculation, looking to tease out waypoints, which we might follow with reliability that may light the way.

In the next chapter, we will examine the role of religion and spiritualism. The endpoints we seek will ultimately lie outside the hard sciences and move into the world of philosophy and spiritualism. Yet we need to understand the tenets of philosophy and the role of truth and evidence on which we will build that foundation. You could say that a marriage between science and the spiritual world has been coming for a very long time. This is particularly so if you consider Eastern spiritualism. However, religion has a role to play here as it has identified the rules of morals and ethics that guide the world's social structures. But more importantly, we need to know what the hard-edged rules of philosophy, truth, and evidence cannot provide to us while examining the meaning of life. For the last ten thousand words of this book, I have taken some effort in laying the foundation of how we might believe. It sounds odd that now I am telling us how we cannot rely on the very elements delivered thus far. This surely seems like a contradiction. This does not change the quest to know the meaning of life, but it does enlarge the arena of possibilities in a way which many will find enlightening.

In the end, we will need to expand the current limits of how we think and look far beyond what we have been taught about reality. For this, we will have to contrast our ways of knowing between traditional modes of thinking and some rather creative alternatives. To do this, without relying on pure faith, we can use the basic structures of philosophy, truth, and evidence in a backdoor sort of way just to keep our feet firmly on the ground. All new knowledge begins with speculation and pure thought of what might be. The acquisition of new knowledge requires that we go beyond the safety of what is certain and comfortable. We must literally consider a new worldview each time new knowledge is acquired. To this end, let us now examine what the principal obstacle is to the consideration of ideas outside our worldview. It is the ego.

Let me provide you with a hypothetical example. How did life begin? The clear majority of us have been taught by our world religions that God created life, through some variation of the Biblical or sacred accounts. This varies from faith to faith, but there is a common thread that runs through the story. I won't go into the details of the various accounts, but in a very general way, they are all the same. Science, however, takes a more pragmatic approach and requires a mechanism of action that is not ascribed to divine intervention. So far there are several theories, but all entail the coming together of the right chemical agents and energy. Some say that this happened as lightning struck a pool of primeval soup. Other theories say that life started in deep oceanic trenches where volcanic action provided the needed energy. Another theory postulates that life arrived on Earth delivered by meteors. The latest theory has life beginning in stages, over thousands or millions of years, as a result of volcanic action delivering energy as heat to pools of water, rich in its chemistry. None of these theories have replicated life but some have produced the precursors needed for life. Many scientists believe that it is only a matter of time before success is found. For now, let us imagine that one day soon one of the laboratories involved in the experimentation succeeds. No doubt religion would rush to respond to this discovery by announcing that was done by God. All the Biblical stories will have been nothing more than metaphors for what really happened. But after such a theoretical discovery, we could create life whenever we wanted! No doubt many would declare their faith unchanged. Yet, for many others, this would change their worldview or, if nothing more significant, greatly expand it.

This is an example of what this book intends to explain in a logical, non-divine manner.

RELIGION

Every religion is good that teaches man to be good; and I know of none that instructs him to be bad.

—Thomas Paine

FOR ALL ENLIGHTENED MINDS, IT IS ESSENTIAL TO BE curious about all things which motivate our personal, moral, and ethical actions. This is how we grow.

Thus, one of the basic questions arises regarding why we, as individuals, choose a particular religious or spiritual point of view?

Where does our sense of morality come from? Have you ever wondered about it? Traditionally, philosophers and others suggest that we are born with a mind's arrow which points in the direction of religiosity or spiritualism, or rather, as has been more recently posited, it resides in our genes.

According to researchers from the universities of Coventry and Oxford, the answer is neither of those is correct. Research points in another direction, our choice of religion and the spiritual views do not enter the world with us from the womb but are a function and benefit of the culture we are born into." According to this point of view, the brain, at birth, is a blank slate, and it is the culture into which we are born that selects our religion.

This is what Richard Darkens (world-renowned biologist) has to say about a very early childhood belief. "The 'beliefs' of four-year-old children? Did it not occur to this spokesperson that children who are too young to realize the importance of 'their' beliefs might also be too young to *possess* those same beliefs in the first place? How can the 'beliefs' of a four-year-old child be 'important' to her if she doesn't even know what her beliefs are.": (Dawkins 2015)

Such research leads to the conclusion that we are not born religious.

However, an important question, with an even broader scope, is why do humans, throughout time and across all cultures, display a propensity to acquire religious, spiritual, or mystical formats to guide behavior, or simply put, why do we believe? Mary neurologists speculate that it is a fool's errand to try to untangle this mystery and one deserves what vociferous arguments they will receive for positing such a quandary. For the believer, this question makes no sense and will serve only to aggravate him or her. From their religious or spiritual perspective, who cares why we believe. At this point, I myself am happy and content to respectfully accept their perspective. For whatever phycological (or other) reason, religion and spirituality have much to recommend to them. Our world is and has always been, a dangerous, unforgiving, and stressful place. Survival both physically and emotionally has never been easy. Yesterday, our ancestors were literally prey for other bigger carnivores looking for meals. Today, we stress over survival in different ways according to our social, economic, or political place on the food chain. If getting and keeping a job isn't challenging enough, trying to stay happy and satisfied with that job is a lifelong challenge. Making ends meet with what your job provides can take you to the threshold of panic. Times are changing all over the world; in the U.S., things never been so polarized and we are the victims of that polarization. At the middle and lower end of the spectrum, which leads to true prosperity, we feel as if we will be blown whichever way the wind meets us with a certain ferocity.

So where do we turn for the hope of some eventual reward? It can only be religion and spirituality which are untarnished by the hand of the state, society, or greed, or so we hope. Here we are safe in the arms of a loving God (or other great forces) whom we don't always understand, but this is who we love and trust when our social structure says "sorry we either can't or won't help you." More importantly, this physical and mental place of worship and belief gives us the under-pinning of social justice, laws, and tenets to guide our lives. They give form and adhesion to the community. It is true that some gods are sometimes demanding and strict, but within the context of the believer's point of view, these agents are only rewarding the faithful and punishing the wicked.

No matter what this world delivers us into, we believe in a life hereafter, and we can trust that for once and for all, justice will be served. This is a very powerful thought and during the worst times of our life, it is the one thing most of us can cling to. You can easily conjure instances throughout history, and across all cultures, where this was the only thing that kept us going, no matter how barbarous the oppressor was and make no mistake of it, there have been many.

Think of the way religion/spirituality supports us. It gives us a firm grounding with regard to the present and the future. It supplies the social and spiritual scaffolding to build our lives. It is religion/ spirituality which are the adhesive binding our like-minded groups together, and they teach morals and ethics that inform us about our spiritual history and gives roots to mankind. Religion/spirituality provides a background to teach our children about the fact there is more than ourselves out there. Religion/spirituality makes the plain sacred, blessing new adventures like marriage and childbirth, and other monumental individual and group undertakings. Religion/ spirituality gives us essential guidelines on how to live with our neighbors, and provides us with rules of sacred conduct. Religion/ spirituality shows us how to reach out and help those who are less fortunate, here and in far off places. Religion/spirituality gives the universe we live in a reason and mechanism for existing. Finally, it provides forgiveness for our trespass; it provides so much more.

The Nature of Faith

There is one more important subject we must address before we leave the topic of the benefits of religion and spirituality. This is the subject of "faith versus fact." This is an emotionally charged topic for most adherents since they believe their religious or spiritual worldview, or some variation of it, in fact, is the only true viewpoint. While I realize that in the eyes of the believers this must be so, it creates amongst all traditions an unsolvable paradox. All religions at once cannot be the true religion or provide the spiritual truth. This question can only have one outcome, and that is that no religion or spiritual belief is a fact or the true path. While they are all immensely helpful, they are mistaken in assuming that only one truth is available. We must be flexible and tolerant. The existence of God, or Tao, or any other supreme agent, cannot be proved using any of the aforementioned techniques in the preceding chapters. Religion and spirituality reside in a different magisterium and two can never be mixed to justify the tenets of the other. That would be an absurdity, although some have tried.

The only logical choice is to accept the matters of core belief and tenets of religion and spirituality on faith. There is nothing negative about this principle, it is just a fact, and adherents are free to go on believing in their worldview so long as they accept that they do so predicated on faith. There is no argument based on acrobatic concepts, clever wording, or anything else, that can prove conclusively that God exists or that there is one true religion. It is purely a matter of faith. Such is the nature of my belief. However, the inescapable reality is that no matter how closely held the belief is, it cannot be proved on fact but only on faith. In the final analysis, choosing faith as the final arbiter of any belief system is a conscientious choice to choose unadulterated opinion (shall we call it sacred opinion?), and not to accept undisputed facts as grounds for a particular opinion.

Beliefs using faith cannot be substantiated by fact and cannot meet the stringent rules of evidence mentioned in the earlier chapter.

Let us now turn to the less benign characteristics of religion and spiritualism. The general view is that most typical adherents of religion or spirituality live happy, peaceful, and tolerant lives. However, this is not always the case. Human history is replete with stories of complete bigotry and hatred for those considered as nonbelievers by one religious or spiritual group over another. This is no modern phenomenon. Humans are innately tribal. The archeological record is clear on this matter. At the beginning (no matter which histology you use), the basic building block of humanity was the family. The origin, notwithstanding many religious or spiritual traditions and texts, is shrouded in mystery. All the social/scientific models cannot pinpoint the original time or name of the first family, though some have tried. But it is reasonable to assume that there must have been a first family to get the whole thing started. We should keep in mind that the actual process may have sprung up in several locations and times only to fail, go extinct, and then start again at another time and place. Such are the fits and starts of history. At any rate, the coalescing process eventually took root, and the first permanent family(ies) was born.

From there, the next step in the evolution of the family was the group or clan. Members were either born into the family(clan) or were captured in war or conjugation of two members of different clans took place. At this stage, the joining of two or more clans formed a tribe.

Some who study this form of social evolution say that group organization came next and is described as a loose confederation of tribes as war allies or trade partners including the social intermixing of individuals. From this loose confederation, the state was born consist-ing of a solid of social/economic/political structure, from which eventually the grand and small civilizations sprang forth, contain-ing all the elements of its precursors. This building of hierarchy is necessarily nebulous because it is the conjuring of experts in the field of social genealogy. So, one expert's genius is another's a heretic. But, for purposes of the story, let's accept it with the knowledge that we can always modify our belief as better information comes along.

For the purposes of this book, civilization has one major flaw, it carries the meme(s) (a meme is an idea, behavior, or style that spreads from person to another person within a culture like a mental virus.) The individuals themselves display a vast number of traits, some admirable and some not so much. But one of the most potent traits goes back to the culture of the family and clan and that is the inherent desire to protect the family via control of essential life-giving and sustaining assets such as food, water, shelter, territory, independence, and reproductive rights. Humans (and other animals) will fight with their very lives to protect this. But it is a fact that resources are limited and so protecting them and their constituents involve protecting them from all those who are not part of "us." Those that are not "us," there-fore become "them." Is this not the root (along with old-fashioned ignorance) of what we call bigotry?

Civilizations have had their share of religious, spiritual, polit-ical, and social bigots over the span of history. Of this, there is no doubt. The Merriam-Webster dictionary labels a bigot as "a person who is obstinately or intolerantly devoted to his or her 'or their' own opinions and prejudices; especially one who regards or treats other members of a group with hatred and intolerance."

Let's look at religious and spiritual bigots.

It appears to be a common idea that the greatest wars have been religious wars, in which the most heinous and outrageous crimes against humanity have been carried out. One can point to the current problems concerning radical Islam, the Croat–Bosnian war, or farther back in time to the crusades pitting the Latin Church against Muslim rule. We might also consider the inquisition as an internal war between the Catholic church against other people who had different religious ideals; this was a war of Christians against (primarily) Christians. We may also think of the Israel vs Arab conflict (wars) as a religious war(s), though strictly speaking it is not. Consider for a moment that the above is only true in a limited way and, more to the point, is that the phenomenon is relatively recent and is largely a Western concept. Take war as a whole, along with human civilization's history, and we find that most wars have not had major religious components to them. If we review the ancient times between 1457 BC and 455 AD, we will find that the most prominent battles, across the globe, were about sixty-three in total. The Battle of Megiddo in 1457 BC was a war that pitted ancient Egypt against Cainites vassal states and was fought over territory. The last of the greatest battles (considered in ancient times) was in 455 AD, known as the Sack of Rome by the Vandals (eastern European-Germanic tribes), and was also a war of conquest, not religion. During that 1912 years, nearly all major battles were not religious at all. They were fought as political and/or territorial wars of conquest. Of course, we cannot deny that there was some religious or spiritual component involved, but we can say it was clearly subordinate to the major motivations.

Historically speaking, the term "religious war" was not even adopted until medieval times, and then only by the western world, this was between the fifth and the sixteenth century. The crusades were actually a number of religious/military campaigns that lasted about two hundred years. These were religious war with the Muslims and the Christen (Latin Church) and the Outremer (the Crusading States) pitted against each other. The significant wars of the twelfth and nineteenth centuries claimed about 160 million lives by some accounts. I have listed them here in order to provide some scope of the number of wars and deaths have been since 1860. They are listed in the order of date, name, and number of deaths:

1860–65: USA civil war (628,000)

1886–1908: Belgium–Congo Free State (8 million)

1898: USA–Spain and the Philippines (220,000)

1899–1902: British–Boer war (100,000)

1899–1903: Colombian civil war (120,000)

1899–1902: Philippines vs USA (20,000)

1900–01: Boxer rebels against Russia, Britain, France, Japan, and USA (35,000)

1901–32: Saudis vs Arabian kingdoms (no number given)

1903: Ottomans vs Macedonian rebels (20,000)

1904: Germany vs Namibia (65,000)

1904–05: Japan vs Russia (150,000)

1910–20: Mexican revolution (250,000)

1911: Chinese Revolution (2.4 million)

1911–12: Italian-Ottoman war (20,000)

1912–13: Balkan wars (150,000)

1915–23: Ottoman genocides (1.2 million Armenians, 500,000 Assyrians, 350,000 Greek Pontians, and 480,000 Anatolian Greeks)

1914–18: World War I (20 million)

1916: Kyrgyz revolt against Russia (120,000)

1917–21: Soviet revolution (5 million)

1917–19: Greece vs Turkey (45,000)

1918–20: Russian civil war (1 million)

1919–21: Poland vs Soviet Union (27,000)

1928–37: Chinese civil war (2 million)

1931: Japanese Manchurian War (1.1 million)

1932–33: Soviet Union vs Ukraine (10 million)

1932: "La Matanza" in El Salvador (30,000)

1932–35: "Guerra del Chaco" between Bolivia and Paraguay (117.500)

1934: Mao's Long March (170,000)

1936: Italy's invasion of Ethiopia (200,000)

1936–37: Stalin's purges (7–13 million)

1936–39: Spanish civil war (600,000)

1937–45: Japanese invasion of China (500,000)

1939–45: World War II (55 million) including holocaust and Chinese revolution

1946–49: Chinese civil war (1.2 million)

1946–49: Greek civil war (50,000)

1946–54: France–Vietnam war (600,000)

1947: Partition of India and Pakistan (1 million)

1947: Taiwan's uprising against the Kuomintang (30,000)

1948–1958: Colombian civil war (250,000)

1948–1973: Arab–Israeli wars (70,000)

1949: Indian Muslims vs Hindus (20,000)

1949–50: Mainland China vs Tibet (1,200,000)

1950–53: Korean war (3 million)

1952–59: Kenya's Mau-Mau insurrection (20,000)

1954–62: French–Algerian war (368,000)

1958–61: Mao's "Great Leap Forward" (38 million give or take)

1960–90: South Africa vs Africa National Congress (no number given)

1960–96: Guatemala's civil war (200,000)

1961–98: Indonesia vs West Papua/Irian (100,000)

1961–2003: Kurds vs Iraq (180,000)

1962–75: Mozambique Frelimo vs Portugal (10,000)

1962–75: Angolan FNLA and MPLA vs Portugal (50,000)

1964–73: USA–Vietnam war (3 million)

1965: Second India–Pakistan war over Kashmir

1965–66: Indonesian civil war (250,000)

1966–69: Mao's "Cultural Revolution" (11 million?)

1966–2016: Colombia's civil war (200,000)

1967–70: Nigeria–Biafra civil war (800,000)

1968–80: Rhodesia's civil war (no number given)

1969: the Philippines vs the communist Bagong Hukbong Bayan/New People's Army (40,000)

1969–79: Idi Amin, Uganda (300,000)

1969–02: IRA—Norther Ireland's civil war (3,000)

1969–79: Francisco Macias Nguema, Equatorial Guinea (50,000)

1971: Pakistan–Bangladesh civil war (500,000)

1972–2014: Philippines vs Muslim separatists (Moro Islamic Liberation Front, etc.) (150,000)

1972: Burundi's civil war (300,000)

1972–79: Rhodesia/Zimbabwe's civil war (30,000)

1974–91: Ethiopian civil war (1,000,000)

1975–78: Menghitsu, Ethiopia (1.5 million)

1975–79: Khmer Rouge, Cambodia (1.7 million)

1975–89: Boat people, Vietnam (250,000)

1975–87: civil war in Lebanon (130,000)

1975–87: Laos' civil war (184,000)

1975–2002: Angolan civil war (500,000)

1976–83: Argentina's military regime (20,000)

1976–93: Mozambique's civil war (900,000)

1976–98: Indonesia–East Timor civil war (600,000)

1976–2005: Indonesia–Aceh (GAM) civil war (12,000)

1977–92: El Salvador's civil war (75,000)

1979: Vietnam–China war (30,000)

1979–88: The Soviet Union invades Afghanistan (1.3 million)

1980–88: Iraq–Iran war (435,000)

1980–92: Sendero Luminoso—Peru's civil war (69,000)

1984: Kurds vs Turkey (35,000)

1981–90: Nicaragua vs Contras (60,000)

1982—90: Hissene Habre, Chad (40,000)

1983: Sri Lanka's civil war (70,000)

1983–2002: Sudanese civil war (2 million)

1986: Indian Kashmir's civil war (60,000)

1987: Palestinian Intifada (4,500)

1988–2001: Afghanistan civil war (400,000)

1988–2004: Somalia's civil war (550,000)

1989–2003: Liberian civil war (220,000)

1989: Uganda vs Lord's Resistance Army (30,000)

1991: Gulf War—large coalition against Iraq to liberate Kuwait (85,000)

1991–97: Congo Kinshasa's civil war (800,000)

1991–2000: Sierra Leone's civil war (200,000)

1991–2009: Russia–Chechnya civil war (200,000)

1991–94: Armenia–Azerbaijan war (35,000)

1992–96: Tajikistan's civil war (50,000)

1992–96: Yugoslavian wars (260,000)

1992–99: Algerian civil war (150,000)

1993–97: Congo Brazzaville's civil war (100,000)

1993–2005: Burundi's civil war (200,000)

1994: Rwanda's civil war (900,000)

1995: Pakistani Sunnis vs Shiites (1,300)

1995: Maoist rebellion in Nepal (12,000)

1998: Congo Kinshasa/Zaire's war—Rwanda and Uganda vs Zimbabwe, Angola, and Namibia (3.8 million)

1998–2000: Ethiopia-Eritrea war (75,000)

1999: Kosovo's liberation war—NATO vs Serbia (2,000)

2001: Afghanistan's liberation war—USA &; the UK vs Taliban (40,000)

2001: Nigeria vs Boko Haram (20,000)

2002: Cote d'Ivoire's civil war (1,000)

2003–11: Second Iraq–USA war—USA, UK, and Australia vs Saddam Hussein's regime and Shiite squads and Sunni extremists (160,000)

2003–09: Sudan vs JEM/Darfur (300,000)

2004: Sudan vs SPLM & Eritrea (number not given)

2004: Yemen vs Houthis (no number given)

2004: Thailand vs Muslim separatists (6,500)

2007: Pakistan vs Pakistani Taliban (38,000)

2011: Iraq's civil war after the withdrawal of the USA (150,000)

2012: Syria's civil war (320,000)

2013: ISIS in Syria, Iraq, Libya (no number given)

2013–15: South Sudan vs rebels (10,000)

2014–16: Ukraine's civil war (9,500)

As I have previously mentioned, an overwhelming number of these wars were not religious wars, but wars of territorial conquest, political/ethnic related, or wars to control vital resources. So, we see the claim that most wars of direct religious nature are primarily a myth.

Thus far we have addressed religious wars, but how about spiritual wars? Do they happen? Do Buddhist wage war?

In the 1970s, nationalist Buddhist monks like Phra Kittiwuttho argued that killing communists did not violate any of the Buddhist precepts. The militant side of Thai Buddhism became prominent again in 2004 when a Malay Muslim insurgency renewed in Thailand's deep south.

Myanmar (old Burma) had become a stronghold of Buddhist aggression and such acts were spurred by hardliner nationalistic monks. The oldest militant organization active in the region is the Democratic Karen Buddhist Army (DKBA), headed by a Buddhist monk U Thuzana, since 1992. In recent years, the monks, and the terrorist acts, are associated with the nationalist 969 movement, particularly in Myanmar and neighboring nations. The violence reached prominence in June 2012 when more than 200 people were killed and around 100,000 were displaced. As of 2012, the 969 movement by monks (prominent among whom is Wirathu) had helped create anti-Islamic nationalist movements in the region and have urged Myanmar Buddhists to boycott Muslim services and trades, resulting in persecution of Muslims in Burma by Buddhist-led mobs. (Wikipedia 2020)

The *Mahabharata* is an ancient Indian epic where the main story revolves around two branches of a family—the Pandavas and the Kauravas—who, in the Kurukshetra war, a battle for the throne of Hastinapura. Interwoven into this narrative are several smaller stories about people dead or living, and philosophical discourses. Krishna-Dwaipayana Vyasa, himself a character in the epic, composed it; according to tradition, he dictated the verses and Ganesh (The Elephant God) wrote them down. At 100,000 verses, it is the longest epic poem ever written, generally thought to have been composed in the 4th century BCE or earlier. The events in the epic play out in the Indian subcontinent and surrounding areas. It was first narrated by a student of Vyasa at a snake-sacrifice of the great-grandson of one of the major characters of the story. Included within it is the *Bhagavad Gita*, which is one of the most important texts of ancient Indian, indeed of world literature. The story of Arjuna, the fabled bowman of the *Mahabharata*, brings out Lord Krishna's view of the war in the *Gita*.

The epic battle of Kurukshetra is about to begin. Krishna drives Arjuna's chariot, drawn by white horses, into the center of the battlefield between the two armies. This is when Arjuna realizes that many of his kinsmen and old friends are among the ranks of the enemy and is appalled by the fact that he is about to kill those he loves. He is unable to stand there any longer, refuses to fight, and says that he does not "desire any subsequent victory, kingdom, or happiness." Arjuna questions, "How could we be happy by killing our own kinsmen?"

Krishna, in order to persuade him to fight, reminds him that there is no such act as killing. He explains that the "atman" or the soul is the only reality; the body is simply an appearance; its existence and annihilation are illusory.

And for Arjuna, a member of the Kshatriya or the warrior caste, fighting the battle is "righteous." It is a just cause and to defend it is his duty or dharma.

"...if you are killed (in the battle) you will ascend to heaven. On the contrary, if you win the war you will enjoy the comforts of an earthly kingdom. Therefore, get up and fight with determination ... With equanimity towards happiness and sorrow, gain and loss, victory and defeat, fight. This way you will not incur any sin.

—*The Bhagavad Gita*

Krishna's advice to Arjuna forms the rest of the *Gita*, at the end of which, Arjuna is ready to go to war.: (Wikipedia 2020)

We can see here that the Hindu tradition does contain a worldview that war is to be avoided, instead, it is to be tolerated for the greater good. This is not so different from many cultural viewpoints throughout human history. It is important to note that this great battle was not fought over religious or spiritual issues. The fact is that although all religious or spiritual traditions have individuals who have promoted war, no religious or spiritual culture contains war as a positive precept. There have been cultures that have been warlike, but these are few between. This may be difficult to understand, particularly in the Abrahamic religions or Judaism's old testimony where God, on many occasions, seemed vengeful and violent, or in early Christianity during the Jewish pogroms of Jew on the way to the Crusades.

The history of Muslims, similar to that of many other communities, is not devoid of violence and warfare. There have been almost perpetual wars, conflicts, and attending violence in the Muslim world. During the Prophetic era, in the Madinah period, the Prophet was at war with all those who fought the nascent Muslim community and the Islamic polity. In the post-prophetic era, the conflicts continued on two fronts. The Islamic polity, which from the beginning was on a pluralistic foundation, continued to be drawn to war with other great civilizations and lesser powers of the time.

Carl Clausewitz had many aphorisms of which the most famous is this: "War is the continuation of politics by other means." So, this seems especially true for religion and spirituality, and mankind along with its institutions. My final take on the question of the fidelity of religion and spirituality, to the role of human goodness and dignity, is that God/the agent is innocent and that it is men who usurp and corrupt his sacred traditions. Let us leave this sobering subject to explore the essence of the Eastern spiritual worldview.

SPIRITUALISM

Re-examine all you have been told.
Dismiss what insults your soul.

—Walt Whitman

WE WILL NOW LEAVE BEHIND WESTERN-STYLE RELI-
gions, the Abrahamic religions, with their one God, the concepts
of heaven and hell as places of reward and punishment, sin and the
traditional Western God as the arbiter of who gets what in the end.
Please note that I am not discounting these religions in any manner,
only setting them aside for a moment to make space to look at other
viewpoints. This ability to consider other perspectives serves a sign-
post on the way to wisdom.

Demographers inform us that there are a little over 7.5 billion
human beings on this planet. Of those, the Abrahamic (tracing their
origin back to the Biblical Abraham) religions account for about 3.6
billion (54 percent) people. The religions, primarily located in the

Middle East, number about one billion (13.4 percent). Buddhists account for half a billion (5.9 percent), indigenous folk religions 0.4 billion (6.4 percent). Interestingly, 23 percent of people exhibit no religious preference. "Convinced" atheists come in at 13 percent, which is about 910,000. As you can see, most of the world believes in some preeminent agent, mostly called God (gods). The major bulk of world religion, 54 percent share some commonalities within their teachings. Those listed below, however, are not all, but a rough list:

1. Monotheism (a single God who is supreme) or demigods which are the manifestation of the one God

2. A personal after-life

3. Sin or transgression

4. Absolution of sin

5. Reward and punishment and a place to receive either

6. Prayer and beseeching

7. Interaction with the deity(s)

8. Spiritual text of the rules of deportment is both personal and communal

9. Leaders who interpret in matters of faith

Let us now examine other schools of thought that take a distinctly different view on some of these important structural points. I will highlight two Eastern spiritual systems that clearly illustrate shifts away from traditional Western concepts and worldviews. These will be Hinduism and Buddhism. Thousands of books have been written on their rich heritage and practices. So, should you need more insight, please consult their place of worship, the local library, or the Internet.

I personally consider (and prefer) Zen Buddhism, an offshoot of the tradition of Indian and Chinese Buddhism. The Japanese give Zen their own flavor, and although the basics are the same, the Japanese have given the practice of Buddhism a decidedly human approach. What does Zen mean? The word Zen is the Japanese pronunciation of the Chinese *Ch'an* which means "meditation." *Ch'an* came to Japan and became Zen around the eighth century. Today, the word Zen is more generally used in the West.

What are the characteristics of Zen Buddhism?

Zen is a stripped-down, determined, uncompromising, cut-to-the-chase, meditation-based Buddhism that takes no interest in doctrinal refinements. While Zen does have some written scriptures, it's primary focus is verified by personal experience and is passed on from master to disciple, hand to hand, ineffably, through stringent, intimate training. Though Zen recognizes, at least loosely, the validity of normative Buddhist scriptures, it has created its own texts over the generations. Liberally flavored with doses of Taoism, Confucianism, and Chinese poetry; written in informal language, studded with Chinese folk sayings and street slang, much of classical Zen literature is built on legendary anecdotes of the great masters. The Buddha is rarely mentioned.

The Eastern traditions such as Hinduism does have a God, in addition to minor gods, many avatars or personalities, within the religious pantheon. The practice of the Hindu faith consists of Shiva, Brahma, Vishnu, and Shakti, and has its closest analog in the Roman

Catholic Trinity. The Hindus believe in reincarnations (and not necessarily returning in human form) until a state called *moksha* is reached, after many cycles of death and re-birth. The religious texts are identified as the Vedas. Some scholars place Hinduism as the world's first major religion at 3500 BCE.

Buddhists seek to reach a state of *nirvana*, following the path of the Buddha, Siddhartha Gautama, who went on a quest for Enlightenment around the sixth century BC. Siddhartha did attain enlightenment. His follower called him the Buddha. We may note that the Buddha never considered himself a god. In fact, there is no belief in a personal god within the teaching. Buddhists believe nothing is fixed or permanent and a change is always possible. (BBC 2009) The teachings of Buddha spread across India, North toward Tibet, and then into China and the rest of Asia. Buddhism focuses on personal spiritual growth through contemplation and meditation. The adherent strives to reach a state of *nirvana* (nirvana is the highest state which someone can attain, a state of enlightenment, meaning that a person's individual desires and suffering dissolve into nothingness). They believe in impermanence as the perpetual state of life and a state of suffering which affects all those who live. Buddhism is the seventh-largest faith in the world.

Now, with the conclusion of this short introduction, I am going to concentrate on the discussion of Taoism which comes to us from China. Taoism, as a religion, began in the year 142 BCE, with the revelation of the Tao to Zhang Daoling or Chang Tao-ling by the personified god of the Tao, Taishang Laojun (Lao Tzu), the highest venerable lord. Zhang Daoling became the first celestial master and founder of the first organized Taoist school of thought. https://www.bbc.co.uk/religion/religions/taoism/history/history.shtml.

It should be noted the Taoism has no official beginning date and grew out of indigenous, traditional spiritual ideas and philosophies. Remember, in its contemporary meaning, the Tao is not a religion in the Western sense.

I am focusing on Taoism because I consider the teachings to be the closest to one important element in my own belief system. The primary difference between my beliefs and the classical Taoist is that I consider Tao philosophy incomplete in its understanding of existence. In short, I feel Taoism does not go far enough. Adherents say that the Tao is unknowable, but here we part company. I believe that we can intuitively understand everything!

The word Tao means "path or way." Taoist ethics vary depending on the particular school, but, in general, tend to emphasize *Wu Wei* (action without intention), naturalness, simplicity, spontaneity, and the three treasures: compassion, frugality, humanity, depending on understanding counterintuitive ideas. Taoism maintains a strong focus on the concept of complementary rather than the opposites that exist in Western religions. This quality is most popularly exhibited in the yin-yang (*Taichi*) symbol.

The symbol is not an illustration of opposites but one of inter-connectedness and complementary existence. One form in the *taichi* defines the other and thus allows it to exist as a whole entity. The dark and the light are constantly in a circular motion and flowing into each other, balancing each other. In this way, Taoists do not conceive sin as being able to exist without virtue, they define each other. They are necessary components of each other. Evil must exist so that virtue can exist, and vice versa. So is the case with all complementary phenomena, one cannot exist without the other.

This has profound implications for the concept of original sin and all other sins for that matter. Sin in the Taoist view can only exist when one abandons their natural goodness. Sin is not visited on a person from the outside (therefore, no original sin). Sin and evil are just the complementary and natural sides of righteousness and good. Where virtue is absent, evil is present, and vice versa. Our task is to live in harmony with Tao.

QP (Quantum Physics) strives to understand the fundamental properties of our physical existence and our quantum condition. The Tao attempts to understand and live in harmony within our spiritual lives. In this, it strives for the fundamentals of acquiring wisdom through naturalness, simplicity, and spontaneity, while living with compassion, frugality, and humility.

It is here that the Tao and QP begin to overlap. When we enter the realm of QP, we enter the realm of counterintuitive realities where forces interact and mix in a way that the non-initiated cannot easily understand. We will get into these phenomena a little later when we find that Taoism and other spiritual concepts are co-joined with QP.

At this stage of our journey, we can ask how an ordinary person like you and I, can live in concert with Tao without being a monk? Our lives are real, we have families, jobs, and ordinary problems. The practical demands for the day are ever-present and pressing.

Over time, some Taoist monks have fallen in love, got married, and had children; they were human. They fell sick, at times, were hungry, or became angry or despondent. They had their share of failure and success, fear, and bravery. It is said that one monk worked so hard at being one with Tao, and he became so holy that birds would come and perch on his shoulders. It was only when he truly saw that the Tao was nothing special that he came in true harmony with the Tao and the birds no longer came to him.

The Tao must be one of the easiest spiritual practices to follow because so much of it is just being natural and being a good person. Yes, some things are considered to be the right actions, like eating healthy, exercising, resting well, and practicing acceptance and patience, especially with ourselves. Understandably, the fundamentals are necessary, and finding Taoist teaching is as simple as going to the library, or the Internet. If you wish to get more involved there are Taoist temples in most major cities. There you can take classes and join a meditation group or meditate on your own. Above all, you must search your own mind for learning wisdom, balance, and peace.

While studying the subject you will come to understand that the Tao has no strict dogma to follow, no God waiting to judge you with a promise of heaven or hell, and no expectations from you, except that you find it for yourself by observing the world and following the natural rivers that flow through your life. Taoist do not ask if there is a God because the question is meaningless to them and unproductive as well. They do not become embroiled in questions of life and death because both are the same to them, and are not to be dwelled upon. Time is condensed as it is natural for it to be just one moment, this moment. What matters is that in that one and only moment, you act as you believe there is no other time. It is also important to know that Taoism does not require you to abandon other spiritual beliefs so long as they mesh well with the teachings and practices of the Tao. I know Christians who are devoted but also believe in the teaching of the Tao. They simply live balanced lives.

MOORINGS

Allow yourself to be an anchor,
and anchored by others.

—Asa Don Brown

EVERYTHING YOU HAVE READ SO FAR WAS AIMED AT providing an anchor for the rest of this book. A grand ship requires a solid place to be moored, especially when the metaphorical tide is strong and the tendency to drift is compelling. We have covered quite a bit of intellectual territory so far, so it's important to look back before moving on to make sure our feet are still grounded, as I hope they are.

I have given you a starting point and a simple objective, to look at what you believe in and compare it to what might or might not be true based on some important criteria thus far provided. I don't want you to feel like I am asking you to put your faith in religion, spiritual grounding, or life philosophy aside; the focus of this book is not to challenge your belief system or your faith in general. But you need to recognize that belief in your worldview may be based more on pure faith than on fact and that there are other viewpoints that you might consider enlightening. The belief that traditional religious faith is justified by anecdotes about the holy texts, and the saying of their prophets is not necessarily proof in belief in what may or may not actually be truth, in the absence of such absolute proof as outlined in the previous chapters of this book; it might be advisable to review your credulity in the matter. This line of reasoning does not intend to defile your faith, but to make you recognize that it is just faith, and as deeply and earnestly held it may be, it is also limited. These beliefs may be limited to your life experience up to this point. My belief is that a rational person would not be offended by this point of view, but would be stricken by some curiosity. Otherwise, one would only be proven to be rigidly dogmatic and inflexible. In that case, I suggest that they stop reading this book now.

Generally, as structured and as deeply rooted in history as the study of philosophy might be, it is also not an "absolute truth" in every case, and as much as I wish spiritualism provided a more solid ground, I am afraid it fairs no better.

Existentialism is a tradition of philosophical enquiry that explores the nature of existence by emphasizing experience of the human subject—not merely the thinking subject, but the acting, feeling, living human individual. In the view of the existentialist, the individual's starting point is characterized by what has been called 'the existential angst' (or, variably, existential attitude, dread, etc.), or a sense of disorientation, confusion, or anxiety in the face of an apparently meaningless or absurd world (Wikipedia 2020).

It is the belief that people are searching to find out who and what they are throughout life, as they make choices based on their experiences, beliefs, and outlook. "This is the realm of religion, philosophy, and spiritualism, which is of itself perfectly acceptable too provided it is something which resonates within us and leads to faith. However, I do believe that there is more 'out there,'" as I also believe there always will be.

To be clear, let me summarize and review our communal history starting with *Homo Neanderthals* who buried their dead which formed the evidence of the use of ritual. The use of burial rituals is believed to be evidence of religious activity, and there is no other evidence that religion existed in human culture before humans reached basic behavioral modernity (we started acting as if we had achieved sentience). I have mentioned this religious/spiritual practice as dating back to 40,000 years. If we fast-forward to about 10,000 BCE or so years ago, during the Neolithic period (Neo means new and lithic mean stone) or the new stone age, we begin to find totems, clay figurines of early gods. Note that these totems are of female goddesses, seated on a throne, with two lions' heads to her left and right, possibly signifying that she had a significant (female) role in the group. The sculpture is dated to about 6000 BCE. This is long before any of the Abrahamic religions of the West came into being. Clearly, humankind was well on its way to religious and spiritual practices.

I know we glossed over the evolution of culture, but this time let's take a look at the evolution of religious and spiritual practices. Probably the most logical place to start is asking why did it arise at all?

The earliest Homo sapiens or other human-like precursors to modern humans (we cannot know all of them all as the fossil record is incomplete) acquired a more refined stage of sentience (Sentience is the capacity to feel, perceive, or experience subjectively. Eighteenth-century philosophers used the concept to distinguish the ability to think (reason) from the ability to feel.) and began to think of themselves as individuals apart from the group. Perhaps they wondered deeply about who they were and how they fitted into the whole panorama of life. These people were finely tuned, after millennia of transformation and evolution, to the intricacies of nature. It would not be hard to imagine that they believed that certain natural elements of the world (the wind, the waters, the storms, earthquakes, scarce or abundant food, and water sources, etc.,) had the power to destroy them or reward them. These elements were interwoven into the natural world in which they lived. Today, we see this way of thinking and living reflected in those people we refer to as "natures' people" such as the Yuri people who live in the Amazon basin or the Austronesians of Melanesia (an island close to New Guinea the South Pacific). These peoples had no contact with formal Westerns or Eastern faiths, so like all of our early ancestors, they developed their own faiths based on their imaginations and what they experienced. I believe the root of all religious and spiritual practice can be traced back to humankind's need to explain and make sense of the world (spiced this up with a healthy fear of the unknown) and the evolutionary drive for survival. This survival instinct, which all living things have, fueled the need to fill the void in the psyche created by death. This *Nü Wa* was mysterious to early humans (as it is to some of us today) and one of the first ancient ceremonies developed were formal burials, along with the leaving of gifts (abstemiously) to be used in the journey after death. In the earliest graves, we have found the remains of the dead buried facing the sunrise, perhaps signifying the rebirth of a new day and the deceased. We know other primates and even elephants seem to morn their dead; so, given the evidence, we know with certainty that humans did this.

We also know that humans, like other primates, lived in intricate social and hierarchical societies. This self-organizing instinct gave us a spectrum of leaders and followers of different ranks. The two major groups that evolved were mystical/religious group leaders or political/community-based leaders. It's hard to know when *shaman* (keepers of religious power and knowledge) split from the political leaders (the more practical day-to-day issues of living) of the groups. My guess is that a long process of melding into two distinct professions, each with their own set of authority and power, took place. In many cases, even today, the king or emperor is considered to be a descendant of God like in (Shinto) Japan. In ancient Egypt, the Pharaohs were god/kings. However, even in Egypt, there were orders of high priests as well. Mostly modern societies have abandoned this duel role of god/king the world over, though where tyranny abounds, the line has become blurred at least in the heart of the public if not in the heart of the despot.

All religions and spiritual practices have an origin story for the place we live in (our world) and myths of how we got here. Religion and spiritualism are much older than science. Ancient Mesopotamians had no distinction between rational science and magic. When a person became ill, doctors prescribed magical formulas to be recited as well as medicinal treatments. The earliest medical prescriptions appear in Sumerian during the third dynasty of Ur (c.2112–c.2004 BCE). The most extensive Babylonian medical text, however, is the *Diagnostic Handbook* written by the *Ummânūi or* chief scholar, Esagil-Kin-Apli of Borsippa, during the reign of the Babylonian king Adad-Apla-Idina (1069-1046 BCE). This was centuries before the first purely scientific worldviews took place.

All religions and spiritual practices have their geneses stories. Here are just three examples:

The Australian aborigines' "legend(s) describes only bare land existing in the beginning. There was no life on Earth—no animals, no

plants, no trees, and no humans. *Wandjina*, the creator, brought our ancestors from within the earth and over the seas, and life began.":
(Holloway 2013)

The Norsemen believed that before there was soil, or sky, or any green thing, there was only the gaping abyss of Ginnungagap. This chaos of perfect silence and darkness lay between the homeland of elemental fire, *Muspelheim*, and the homeland of elemental ice, *Niflheim*. Frost from *Niflheim* and billowing flames from *Muspelheim* crept toward each other until they met in Ginnungagap. Amid the hissing and sputtering, the fire melted the ice, and the drops formed themselves into Ymir (Screamer), the first of the godlike but destructive giants. Ymir was a hermaphrodite and could reproduce asexually; when he slept, more giants leaped forth from his legs and from the sweat of his armpits.

As the frost continued to melt, a cow, Audhumla (abundance of humming), emerged from it. She nourished Ymir with her milk, and in turn, was nourished by salt licks in the ice. Her licks slowly uncovered Buri (progenitor), the first of the Aesir tribe of gods. Buri had a son named Bor (son), who married Bestla (perhaps "wife"), the daughter of the giant Bolthorn (Baleful thorn). The half-god, half-giant children of Bor and Bestla were Odin, who became the chief of the Aesir gods, and his two brothers, Vili and Ve. Odin and his brothers slew Ymir and set about constructing the world from his corpse. They fashioned the oceans from his blood, the soil from his skin and muscles, vegetation from his hair, clouds from his brains, and the sky from his skull. Four dwarves, corresponding to the four cardinal points, held Ymir's skull aloft above the earth.

The gods eventually formed the first man and woman, Ask and Embla (Adam and Eve), from two tree trunks, and built a fence around their dwelling-place (the Garden of Eden), Midgard, to protect them from the giants (evil, old age, and death).: (McCoy n.d.)

The Mesoamerican creation myths are attributed to various cultures and civilizations.

According to the story, the two gods decided to preserve their legacy by creating an Earth-bound species looking like them. The first attempt was man made from mud, but Tepeu and Kukulkán found that the mud crumbled. The two gods summoned the other gods, and together they decided to make man from wood. However, since these men had no soul and soon lost loyalty to the creators, the gods destroyed them by rain. Finally, a man was constructed from maize, the Mayans staple, and sacred food. The deity Itzamna is credited as being the creator of the calendar along with creating writing." (Wikipedia 2019)

As you can see, there are vague but distinguishable similarities between these three samples of creation myths. The human mind is vast in its imagination but not inexhaustible, so patterns begin to form. If you go down further with your cultural/historical microscope, you will find that such similarities are evident in the practices that the people performed in both ancient and modern times but with, of course, infinite variations in the details. The idea of a savior is not the exclusive providence of the Abrahamic religions as well.

Glycon

In the middle of the 100s AD, out along the south coast of the Black Sea, Glycon was the son of the God Apollo, who came to Earth through a miraculous birth; was the Earthly manifestation of divinity; came to earth in fulfillment of divine prophecy; gave his chief believer the power of prophecy; gave believers the power to speak in tongues; performed miracles; healed the sick; and raised the dead. (Pagans Origin of the Christ n.d.)

Horus

Born of a virgin, Isis. Only begotten son of the God Osiris. Birth heralded by the star Sirius, the morning star. Ancient Egyptians paraded a manger and child representing Horus through the streets at the time of the winter solstice (about DEC-21). In reality, he had no birth date; he was not a human. Death threat during infancy: Herut tried to have Horus murdered. Handling the threat: The God that tells Horus' mother 'Come, thou goddess Isis, hide thyself with thy child'. An angel tells Osiris's father to 'Arise and take the young child and his mother and flee into Egypt'. (Break in life history: No data between the ages of 12--30. Age at baptism: 30.) The subsequent fate of the Baptist: Beheaded. He walked on water, cast out demons, healed the sick, restored sight to the blind. Was crucified, descended into Hell; resurrected after three days. (Suratwala 2011) Global Conversation 73/11.

Attis

Attis: Born of a Virgin on December 25th, Crucified and Resurrected after Three Days

In many mythicist writings, the ancient Phrygo–Roman god Attis is depicted as having been born of a virgin mother on December 25th, being killed and resurrecting afterwards. Here we shall examine the evidence for these contentions, which parallel the gospel story and Christian tradition concerning Jesus Christ.

- Attis was born on December 25th of the Virgin Nana.

- He was a shepherd, as Christ was called the 'Good Shepherd'.

- He was considered the 'only begotten son', the Logos/Word and the savior slain for the salvation of mankind.

- His cult had a sacrificial meal, at which, it is contended, his body as bread was eaten by his worshippers.

- His priests were 'eunuchs for the kingdom of heaven' (Mt 19:12).

- Attis served as both the Divine Son and the Father.

- On 'Black Friday', he was 'crucified' on a tree, from which his holy blood ran down to redeem the earth.

- He descended into the underworld.

- After three days, Attis was resurrected on March 25th (as tradition held of Jesus) as the 'Most High God'.

You will notice the striking and glaring similarities between the Egyptian Horus and major points in the life of Christ. This is also mirrored in the story of Attis of Phrygia, a Greek city-state. The similarities are so close that they could be the same story co-opted by later faiths. While this may sound blasphemous to some, there is enough historical record to confirm the myths. This is not the only allegory to spring up in other cultures separated by hundreds or thousands of years. For example, many cultures have a cataclysmic flood myth such as the Welsh myth of the flood.

Dwyfan and Dwyfach, sometimes also called Dwyvan and Dwyvach, in Welsh mythology, were the equivalents of Noah or the deputation who take their names from small rivers, as told in a flood legend from the Welsh triads. A great flood was caused by the monster Afanc, who dwelt in Llyn Llion (possibly Bala Lake). All humans were drowned except Dwyfan and Dwyfach, who escaped in a mastless boat. They built an imposing ship (or ark) called *Nefyd Naf Neifion*, on which they carried two of every living kind. From Dwyfan and Dwyfach, the island of Prydain (Britain) was repeopled. Dwyfach appears to take her name from the small Dwyfach (Welsh: little Dwy) river of Gwynedd (until 2018, Caernarvonshire) that flows into Cardigan Bay; Dwyfan would then be derived from the river it enters, the Dwyfawr or Dwyfor (Welsh: great Dwy). A lake monster from Welsh mythology, the Afanc, can also be traced through references in British and Celtic folklore.

Sometimes described as taking the form of a crocodile, giant beaver, or dwarf, it is also said to be a demonic creature. The Afanc was said to attack and devour anyone who entered its waters.

Various versions of the tale are known to have existed. Iolo Morganwg, who revived Welsh bardic traditions during the 18th and 19th centuries, popularized a version of the myth that had Hu Gadarn's two long-horned oxen drag the Afanc from the lake, enabling it to be killed. An earlier variation on this had the oxen cast the Afanc into Llyn Ffynnon Las (lake of the blue fountain), where it was unable to breach its rocky banks to escape.–(Boucher 2019)

Pan Gu and Nü Wa

Long, long ago, when heaven and earth were still one, the entire universe was contained in an egg-shaped cloud. All the matter of the universe swirled chaotically in that egg. Deep within the swirling matter was Pan Gu, a huge giant who grew in the chaos. For 18,000 years, he developed and slept in the egg. Finally, one day he awoke and stretched, and the egg broke to release the matter of the universe. The lighter, purer elements drifted upwards to make the sky and heavens, and the heavier impure elements settled downwards to make the earth. In the midst of this new world, Pan Gu worried that heaven and earth might mix again; so, he resolved to hold them apart, with the heavens on his head and the earth under his feet. As the two continued to be separated, Pan Gu grew to hold them apart. For 18,000 years he continued to grow until the heavens were 30,000 miles (ca. 48,280 km) above the Earth. For much longer, he continued to hold the two apart, fearing the return of the chaos of his youth. Finally, he realized they were stable, and soon after that he died. With the immense giant's death, the earth took on a new character. His arms and legs became the four directions and the mountains. His blood became the rivers, and his sweat became the rain and dew. His voice became the thunder, and his breath became the winds. His hair became the grass, and his veins became the roads and paths. His teeth and bones became the minerals and rocks, and his flesh became the soil of the fields. Up above, his left eye became the sun, and his right eye became the moon. Thus, in death, as in life, Pan Gu made the world as it is today.

Many centuries later, there was a goddess named No Wa who roamed this wild world that Pan Gu had left behind, and she became lonely in her solitude. Stopping by a pond to rest, she saw her reflection and realized that there was nothing like herself in the world. She resolved to make something like herself for company.

From the edge of the pond, she took some mud and shaped it in the form of a human being. At first, her creation was lifeless, and she set it down. It took life as soon as it touched the soil, however, and soon the human was dancing and celebrating its new life. Pleased with her creation, No Wa made more of them, and soon her loneliness disappeared in the crowd of little humans around her. For two days she made them, and still, she wanted to make more. Finally, she pulled down a long vine and dragged it through the mud, and then she swung the vine through the air. Droplets of mud flew everywhere and, when they fell, they became more humans that were nearly as perfect as the ones she had made by hand. Soon she had spread humans over the whole world. The ones she made by hand became the aristocrats, and the ones she made with the vine became the poor common people.

Even then, No Wa realized that her work was incomplete because as her creations died, she would have to make more. She solved this problem by dividing the humans into male and female so that they could reproduce and save her from having to make new humans to break her solitude.

Many years later, Pan Gu's greatest fear came true. The heavens collapsed so that there were holes in the sky, and the earth cracked, letting water rush from below to flood the earth. At other places, fire sprang forth from the earth, and everywhere wild beasts emerged from the forests to prey on the people. Nu Wa drove the beasts back and healed the earth. To fix the sky, she took stones of many colors from the river and built a fire in which she melted them. She used the molten rock to patch the holes in the sky, and she used the four legs of a giant turtle to support the sky again. Exhausted by her labors, she soon lay down to die and, like Pan Gu, from her body came many more features to adorn the world that she had restored.: http://www. gly.uga.edu/railsback/CS/CSPG&NW.html

Again, the striking similarities to human mythology and religious and spiritual legends are not coincidental. These myths are not an accident of history. This borrowing happens too often to be so coincidental. The history of man is one of constant migration across the globe, and of the migrants taking the myths/stories of their culture with them when they traveled. These stories have themes embedded within them which resonated with the host culture and so, over time, they have been absorbed and embellished into their mythology. Finally, the new mythology becomes so entrenched in the local culture and religious history that it becomes known as "truth." This may well be the mechanism that gives us the foundations of faith we have today.

Religion and spirituality did not pop into existence when one holy prophet or another just happened to come along. The development evolved over millennia, born of natural curiosity and wonder of mankind, starting with the individual and expanding outward within each social unit until a constellation of beliefs, slowly but inexorably, coalesced into the vast web of such practices as we see today. Under this principle, there can be no one true religion of spiritual practice. This web of religious and spiritual outlooks is local and temporal in nature and depends on the place and time of its genesis. Thus, this is a personal pantheism that depends more on circumstance than on your current faith and its history. This not to devalue any faith, but to put it into a historical and cultural perspective. Religion and spirituality form the bedrock of society throughout the world historically. We should be grateful for the institutions that inform us and give us a moral foundation. But we must also understand the history of this foundation and keep that in perspective. This view, when truly understood, leads to tolerance and enlightenment, and is perhaps the greatest gift.

The reason I provided all this information was to give you a broad idea of where our religions, spiritual practices, legal practices, and science and philosophies originate, and to find their roots. Each culture (ancient and modern) has developed systems and practices that have a carry-over effect on current practices. It took thousands of years and countless generations of trial and error to develop the underpinnings and social structures that help to create the practices we use today. It has been a long evolutionary process that laid down the groundwork concerning how we pray, what we believe in, the development of the laws we follow, and the science we use. These are our moorings that hold our metaphorical ship in place.

SCIENCE

*Ideas are like stars; you will not succeed in touching
them with your hands. But like the seafaring man on the
desert of waters, if you choose them as your guides, and
follow them you will reach your destiny.*

—Carl Schurz (1829–1906)

I WAS NOT ABLE TO FIND A DEFINITIVE WORD THAT
succinctly covers what we could call the uppermost classes of knowledge. I was looking for a sort of taxonomical phase that I could use
to subsume religion, spiritualism, philosophy, science (and perhaps
metaphysics). I was not able to find such a classification system, so I
will borrow the one from natural taxonomy (the formal system of the
classification of living things) and collectively call them "domains."
Please remember this is just my convention adopted for use in this
book. This is an important distinction because I will maintain, in a
broad sense, that these domains have nothing to say regarding each

other. As a result, science cannot authoritatively comment on religion and vice versa. We will inspect this assertion a little later.

One domain trying to comment on another is like having a pearl comment on a cloud, the two do not have anything to say about the other in an intelligent manner. There may be elements that are present in one or more domains, but this is only in a loose tangential way. You could say that the shadow of one domain falls across the shadow of another, such is the condition of coincidence. Today, scholars and learned individuals tend to specialize in their respective domains. There is so much knowledge out there that one cannot keep up with all there is to know. So, some delve deeper and specialize in sub-domains like a surgeon who specializes in the surgery of the heart or brain. This is the nature of knowledge in any of the root domains. However, it is still possible to have a grasp of multiple domains at once, and we may be justified in calling this person a renaissance thinker. Thinker/practitioners like Leonardo da Vinci comes to mind. Today, such people are called polymaths. James Ashenhurst qualifies as such an individual. He studied mathematical economics, has a PhD in physics, studied with Steve Hawkins, started a software company which was bought by Microsoft, and then founded "Microsoft Research," studied paleontology with specialization in dinosaurs' mating habits, was a prize-winning nature photographer, was master French cook, and founded "Intellectual Ventures," a controversial patent-holding company.

You don't have to be a polymath (one who knows a lot about many subjects), but you do need to be a very curious person. This because it takes a full background of ideas to understand the whole

of what we are attempting to understand. Besides the cross-polli-
nation of concepts and ideas, we must understand how the tenets
of each domain peripherally support or buttresses the concepts of
another. I have already spoken about the basic beliefs of Taoism and
its correlation with QP and quantum mechanics. Further, quantum
mechanics is closely tied to the discipline of mathematics, but Taoism
is only tangentially tied. For now, we will restrict our discussion to
the domain of science, we need a link between it and the field of
philosophy where the nature of truth holds sway; we need to discuss
the subject of truth and how truth intersects with science, that is, how
do we know science is telling us the truth.

It is fundamental to scientific thinking that ideas about scientific
knowledge are ensconced in what are called theories. A theory is not
a fact but an idea that can only be considered true when it has passed
a rigorous test and (using the scientific method) peer reviews. Then
also, it is only considered valid until is it proven (by new knowledge) to be untrue. Scientific knowledge is not set in stone, no matter
how many times it has been challenged and has withstood the tests.
There is no absolute scientific knowledge, there is only the prevail-
ing theory. Some theories such as Einstein's theory of gravity have
been challenged so often and so thoroughly that the common man
thinks of it as fact, but in truth it is still a theory. Mathematics does not
always deal strictly with numbers. It can also deal with concepts. For
example, if A is larger the B, and B is smaller than C, then C must be
smaller than A. This can be expressed as an equation but does not have
to be. Mathematician use equations as a language which have strict
rules governing the use of this language. Additionally, mathematics

is not boundless and does have its limits. Gödel's incompleteness theorems are the name given to two theorems (true mathematical statements), proved by Kurt Gödel in 1931. They are theorems in mathematical logic. Mathematicians once thought that everything that is true has a mathematical proof. A system that has this property is called *complete*; one that does not is called *incomplete*. Also, mathematical ideas should not contain *contradictions*. This means that they cannot be true and false at the same time. A system that does not include contradictions is called *consistent*. Gödel said that "every non-trivial (interesting) formal system is either incomplete or inconsistent: There will always be questions that cannot be answered using a certain set of axioms.

You cannot prove that a system of axioms is consistent unless you use a different set of axioms.

Those theorems are important to mathematicians because they prove that it is impossible to create one set of axioms that explains everything in math."

The point is that all knowledge has limitations, there are always things that we do not know with regard to each domain, and there are always things we cannot know. The difference is that things we do not know may simply be those that we have not discovered the answer to or even the right question that needs to be asked. By contrast, things that we cannot know are things that are simply beyond our ability to know (for now), for example how big is the universe (not just the observable universe).

Earlier I said that perhaps metaphysics was one of the legitimate domains. The reason I included this as a legitimate area of inquiry is that I have a distaste for absolutes. So, to arbitrarily disavow this field as unworthy would be ignorance. Although I have a logical objection to things like "ghosts," I cannot deny that there may be extraterrestrials. For now, I relegate this area mostly, but not exclusively, to "maybe"; the jury is still out. I also said that we would visit the line of reasoning that religion and science can't support each others' universal ways. I am aware that the creationists attempt to usurp science to prove religion, and to have them coexist is the subject and explanation of my prohibition on such tactics and will be addressed below.

One who purports such creationist ideas would make poor scientists. The theory of evolution is one of their favorite targets to scientifically support the Christian creation story. Their espoused point is that God created the world (everything) according to an explicit doctrine based on the Bible. Here we are talking about Western Abrahamic religions. The creationists reject a (traditional, western) non-deity form of evolution. One of the favorite antidotes is the multilayered plea to (misplaced) statistics in the absence of a complete lack of the understanding of evolution. The story goes that if one was to disassemble a 747 jet and leave it in a junkyard and imagine that a hurricane swept through the junkyard and reassembled the parts back into a flyable 747. They claim that the odds against such an outcome are so ridiculous as to be laughable (it is laughable but not statistically impossible if one understands that evolution works over vast spans of time). This a false use of logic and probability theory. This claim is analogous to non-evolution (of and by itself) creating any part of the complex world we see instantaneously. The two examples cannot be overlaid as one has nothing to do with others. That is, the 747 analogy does not take evolutionary time into consideration.

There are several problems with the foundation of this story. First, it assumes that evolution has an intended goal, in this example to create a flyable 747. Evolution has no such intent. Evolution is a random process that uses the materials available to create whatever is created when matter and natural processes are combined over and over again in a never-ending cycle. I do agree with the junkyard idea that the 747 parts would eventually evolve into something. Over time, you could expect the chemical components of the parts of the jet to break down due to the natural processes that they might be subjected to. Depending on the circumstance, they may break down into their elemental chemical constituents. Perhaps in thousands or millions of years, these elemental chemicals would migrate to different parts of the Earth where future generations might harvest them and create some new and useful item(s). Given that humanity lasts for so long, it is possible that the human propensity for creativeness will not only harvest the remnants of the 747 but also turn them into something even more marvelous, perhaps something like a sentient android. Creationist stories start out sounding reasonable, however by the use of clear logical examination they are often found full of flaws. They rely on a misplace reliance on facts which have either be distorted or completely left out.

One of the other stories that the creationists claim, uses the gaps in the paleontological record of fossils remains. Here, the story is that the fossil record should show a smooth and constant record of the evolution of each living thing as it evolved. This, in fact, is a good premise but completely ignores the fact that not all living things have bodies that can fossilize. Soft-bodied creatures generally do not fossilize. Secondly, the process of fossilization requires very specific circumstances which are in fact, extremely rare. Thirdly, their logic does not consider the natural weather patterns of wind, snow, rain, flood, sea-level change, and tectonic activity, or volcanic activity, and other natural processes, which greatly mobilized the Earth (tectonic plates) over millions and millions of years, and scattered or destroyed the potential fossils. In other words, the Earth itself underwent enormous changes over the eons and separated or destroyed many of the rare fossils that did exist. We are indeed lucky to find what we have found. Fossilization takes millions and millions of years. What kind of rational mind would even consider a continuous fossil record to survive?

I am afraid that the plan to tie religion and science together is doomed to failure before it even begins.

Now, there is another tactic used by purveyors of these false thoughts and that is to recruit as many bonified scientists to profess their belief in God as possible. Frankly, I see nothing wrong with religion and spiritualism which are based on faith, this is a truism. However, if a scientist has religious faith, I don't understand what is wrong with that? Depending upon the depth of his faith, his views of some element of scientific evidence may be dampened, but this doesn't prove anything. At best, it can show that scientists can have faith in religious matters and scientific beliefs in scientific matters.

In fact, it will not be surprising if scientists who are closest to knowing the wonderful working of the universe, are the ones to sit and gaze at how magnificent our natural world is. Who they choose to ascribe this wonder to is a matter of personal choice and faith, but it does not make the religious or spiritual point of view the arbiter of what the truth is.

On studying the matter, you will find that the belief in God by scientists is strongest at the level of those who are less educated within the scientific community. When examined, we found that among the notable scientific community, the belief in God drops perceptively; a sample of the National Academy of Scientists has a much low rate of believers. A recent poll shows that 85 percent of the greater scientists reject the Christian God. In the natural scientific community, the number is close to 100 percent. Science resides at a point where human aspirations and practicality meet. As wonderful as faith is, it will not create a cleaner environment, or produce a computer or power grid, or build a bridge, cure worldwide diseases, or feed the hungry. Only science can do those things, perhaps God can influence their progress, but when was the last time someone saw God bailing hay or building an interstellar probe? God may indeed guide our actions, but in the meantime, we must be practical and help ourselves.

Another claim that is sometimes made by religious persons is the belief that a personified God personally created all things. It is claimed that all that there is cannot possibly emerge from nothing (*ex nihilo*).

Emergent behavior is the global (systematic) consequence of local interactions of individuals in the system's population. A pattern in nature is an emergent property because it is the result of a systematic interaction of its component parts. Super-organisms such as bee hives, bird flocks, and coral reefs are complex systems that exhibit unique natural and dynamic patterns that behave in unexpected ways that are not predictable from the behavior of their members. These systems operate as if they have organized themselves. But, in fact, this "self-organization" is an emergent behavior caused by the actions of all individuals within the system acting upon a fixed set of rules. There are no leaders. http://www.patternsinnature.org/Book/EmergentPatterns.html

In philosophy, systems, theory, science, and art, occurs when "the whole is greater than the sum of the parts," meaning that the whole has properties that its parts individually do not have. These properties come about because of natural interactions among the parts.

Emergence plays a central role in the theories of integrative levels and of complex systems. For instance, the phenomenon of life, as studied in biology, is an emergent property of chemistry, and psychological phenomena emerge from the neurological phenomena of living things.

In philosophy, theories that emphasize emergent properties have been called emergentism. Almost all accounts of emergentism include a form of epistemic or ontological irreducibility to the lower levels.

Science has shown us that, in our day-to-day experience, emergent systems are quite common. Take snowflakes, for example, or ice crystals of which snowflake is constructed. A snowflake begins as a high-altitude free-floating speck of dust in which a water molecule coalesces and then it freezes. Other water molecules attach themselves to it and so on, and finally an elaborate snowflake form.

Let's look at another natural phenomenon called "self-organizing" systems. It is interesting as a side note that religion and spiritualism could easily be described as self-organizing systems. Self-organization, also called (in the social sciences) spontaneous order, is a process where some form of overall order arises from local interactions between parts of an initially disordered system. The process is spontaneous, not needing to be controlled by any external agent. It is often triggered by random fluctuations, amplified by positive feedback. The resulting organization is wholly decentralized, distributed over all the components of the system. As such, the organization is robust and able to survive or self-repair substantial perturbations. Chaos theory discusses self-organization in terms of islands of predictability in a sea of chaotic unpredictability. Self-organization occurs in many physical, chemical, biological, robotic, and cognitive systems. Examples of self-organization include crystallization, thermal convection of fluids, chemical oscillation, animal swarming, neural circuits, and artificial neural networks. (Wikipedia 2020)

The idea that the dynamics of a system can lead to an increase in its organization has a long history. Ancient atomists such as Democritus and Lucretius believed that designing intelligence is unnecessary to create order in nature, arguing that given enough time, space, and matter, order emerges by itself. The philosopher René Descartes presents self-organization hypothetically in the fifth part of his 1637 *Discourse on Method*. He also elaborated on the idea in his unpublished work *The World*.

Immanuel Kant used the term "self-organizing" in his 1790 *Critique of Judgment*, where he argued that teleology is a meaningful concept only if there exists such an entity whose parts or organs are simultaneously the ends and the means. Such a system of organs must be able to behave as if it has a mind of its own, that is, it can govern itself.

"In such a natural product as this, every part is thought as owing its presence to the agency of all the remaining parts, and as existing for the sake of the others and the whole, that is as an instrument or organ ... The part must be an organ producing the other parts—each, consequently, reciprocally producing the others ... Only under these conditions and upon these terms can such a product be an organized and self-organized being, and, as such, be called a physical end. (Simpson 1985)

Sadi Carnot (1796–1832) and Rudolf Clausius (1822–88) discovered the second law of thermodynamics in the nineteenth century. It states that "total entropy, sometimes understood as a disorder, will always increase over time in an isolated (closed) system. This means that a system cannot spontaneously increase its order without an external relationship that decreases order elsewhere in the system (e.g., through consuming the low-entropy energy of a battery and diffusing high-entropy heat)."

Eighteenth-century thinkers had sought to understand the universal laws of form to explain the observed forms of living organisms. This idea became associated with Lamarckism and fell into disrepute until the early twentieth century when D'Arcy Wentworth Thompson (1860–1948) attempted to revive it.

The psychiatrist and engineer W. Ross Ashby introduced the term "self-organizing" to contemporary science in 1947. It was taken up by the cybernetics Heinz Foerster, Gordon Pask, Stafford Beer; Foerster organized a conference on "The Principles of Self-Organization" at the University of Illinois, Allerton Park, in June 1960, which led to a series of conferences on self-organizing systems. Norbert Wiener took up the idea in the second edition of his *Cybernetics: Or Control and Communication in the Animal and the Machine* (1961).

Self-organization is the spontaneous often seemingly purposeful formation of spatial, temporal, spatiotemporal structures or functions in systems composed of few or many components. In physics, chemistry, and biology, self-organization occurs in open systems driven away from thermal equilibrium. The process of self-organization can be found in many other fields also, such as economy, sociology, medicine, technology (Haken 2008).

The above review of the discoveries illuminates a scientific understanding of the complex questions that help us understand the blurry veil, caused by the lack of knowledge, which can lead to a clearer understanding of the world around us and the processes within it. The hard sciences, using the scientific method. Thus, the majority of educated persons have come to rely on the lessons that science teaches us. However, it is critical to note that religion and spiritualism do not lend themselves to inquiries based on the scientific method any more than scientific thinking can be adjudicated in the realm of faith. ("Scientific method is an empirical method of knowledge acquisition, which has characterized the development of natural science since, at least, the 17th century, involving careful observation, which includes rigorous skepticism about what is observed, given those cognitive assumptions about how the world works influence how one interprets a percept; formulating hypotheses, via induction, based on such observations; experimental testing and measurement of deductions drawn from the hypotheses; and refinement (or elimination) of the hypotheses based on the experimental findings.)

In actuality, while this chapter directly addresses the role and vitality of "true science," it also contrasts the role of religion and its relationship to science. This contrasting is in no way intended to debunk, or in any way diminish the legitimate and virtuous role religiosity plays in our spiritual life. In the final analysis, it is vital that we recognize that these two are truly separate domains of the human experience.

THE EGO

Lying increases the creative faculties, expands the ego, lessens the friction of social contacts . . . It is only in lies, wholeheartedly and bravely told, that human nature attains through words and speech, the forbearance, the nobility, the romance, the idealism, that—being what it is— It falls so short of in fact and indeed.

—Clare Boothe Luce (1903-87)

WE ARE GOING TO EXPLORE THE EGO FROM A NON-PSY-chological viewpoint, which is a non-classical Freudian outlook, and use a contextual moral perspective to explore the same. I am using this approach to make you understand how the prosaic ego can be a roadblock to understanding what truth is. The ego can mask understanding and obliterate a clear view of the truth.

If I were to say that the ego is both the bane and vigor of our personal identity, this would not be far off the mark. On one hand, a healthy ego can be an excellent survival tool but, on the other, this can render our chances of seeing beyond ourselves completely impossible. The ego, and the message that it broadcasts from us to the world, can be the biggest lie we tell the world but also the darkest secret we keep to ourselves and from ourselves. Yet, without a healthy ego or a strong sense of self-esteem, we may shrivel to nothingness. Humans, like other animals, compete for a place in the hierarchy. This is the social stage on which we perform the drama of life. We constantly measure ourselves against others and show a natural yearning for a higher place on the social ladder. As children we learn to understand and compare what our parents' standing in the community is. A father who is an airline pilot trumps one of a lessor community standing and so it may affect the child's sense of self-worth, as measured against their peers by parental proxy. We feel that this is the true message (due to the ego), yet it does creep around the edges of self-esteem and tugs away at how we perceive ourselves and our peers. Everyone needs to know themselves and be honest with themselves. The ego can only harm you if it is out of balance with your spiritual well-being. There is a definite difference between an unhealthy ego and a healthy sense of self-worth. If this is balanced, and you avoid self-aggrandizement, you are probably safe from an overactive ego.

Ego is a tool that nature provides and, like most such tools, contains survival value at its core. The ego and the concept we ascribe to it are distorted by cultural interpretation and has now become a shorthand for a malicious sense of self-importance. When we change the word ego for self-esteem, its meaning softens and becomes positive. For the sake of this chapter, and in keeping with the spirit of this book, the negative connotation of the ego will be used, especially to contrast it with self-esteem, which is perceived as positive.

As mentioned above, the ego/self-esteem is a survival tool, a piece of mental apparatus that helps us navigate our social landscape and our place in it. This leads to a social hierarchy that helps maintain order and the health of the community. Unfortunately, this also carries negative implications, creating the "haves and the have-nots." Such an ordering is flexible, and all members can move up or down the ladder using social wrangling, and inter-social and intellectual maneuvering. A capable ego/self-esteem obviously plays a big part in our social mobility. One of the purposes of this book is to provide ample opportunity for self-examination. One of its goals is to provide a safe place for you to re-examine who you are, and what and why do you believe in the things you do. Taking a penetrating look inside yourself can nudge you into a new and powerful perspective that, so far, may have been hidden from your worldview. This is a positive step since we all can and need to grow. To achieve this goal, it is important for you to review your own disposition and the effects that it has on your worldview, which is constructed, in great part, by the ego. It is my observation that most persons with strong negative (or quasi-negative) points of view about their fellow man tend to be inflexible and dogmatic about their belief system, and are likely to suffer from an overactive ego. After all, the ego is the voice that tells us we are right, and they are wrong with little or no room for compromise.

So, how does a person go about subjugating the ego? It can be predicted that you will not get much further in your honorable journey without doing so. Let me begin by telling you about my own collision with my ego.

When I was much younger, I considered myself a gifted artist, a creator of unique things. I had many successes where my peers extolled my work. Fortunately, I recognized that my ego pushed me to think "I" was exceptional, maybe more exceptional than I truly was. However, I was left with the nagging feeling that my work was not entirely my own, I felt it came from beyond my own personal capabilities. The work was exemplary, I had to admit, but a feeling kept me thinking that it was not all me. From the time I was a child, I was painfully shy. I knew then that I had difficulties with self-esteem. I was aware of the ego and, quite frankly, it scared me. As a creative person, I began to find ways to identify and diminish an overactive ego. The solution was the creation, in my own mind, of the view that my work was not all mine. I didn't mind because the work spoke for itself and could stand on its own merits, that was enough for me. I could not deny that I did have a hand in its creation. I was fortuitous enough to experience a great *satori*, an "ah-ha" moment. I was able to conceive that I was a lens through which the energy, which is creativity, was focused through and came to be born into the world; my action gave it substance. To this day, this is the mechanism of action I ascribe to all the artists and fellow creators. Now, I can create things and not be troubled by the ego.

I believe that this is how we are. We all have special talents that are exceptional and unique. These represent human purity of thought which accounts for the great accomplishments of our race. You can see how the subjugation of the ego becomes something wonderful and liberating. Our task is to identify, in ourselves, how we measure the amount of power that the ego has over us. The flexibility of our mind is a strong indicator of how well our life is balanced. The moment we accept an idea or concept as dogma, we are being asked to abandon our own identity, our own free will to look at an idea, analyze what we find, and draw on our own intelligence, to see if we are truly acting as free agents of our own mind and spirit. We must always be the total and complete arbiter of what we believe in, but with ego in check.

The ego may enter our unconscious and bring rationalizations based on preconceived bias. And tell us that our choices are a function of our fundamental belief system. This belief system has been in the making for years and is well armored against thoughts that do not fit neatly into the temple of truth that we have created.

I wish I could tell you that neutralizing an entrenched ego is easy or simple, but it's not. It is for this reason that, as soon as you are aware of its corrosive effects, you must intercede with mental and spiritual discipline. You must teach yourself, every day, to practice self-discipline. Tend to the details, particularly the ones that are small but difficult for you. Do the little things and do them in small increments. The road to truth is long and difficult and doing the wise thing consistently only comes with practice; patience is essential to acquire and promote self-discipline.

The ego will be there, waiting for you, giving you a nudge to do what your ego wants, and not what is best for you. The arguments, because they come from within as part of a preconceived worldview, will be strong. At this point, you will need the self-discipline to question your own motives. It is said that you cannot know what you do not know. In the case of the ego, the situation is more insidious, because your ego is telling you that you absolutely know what you do not know. It takes a strong will and great spiritual flexibility and fortitude to challenge your own preconceived ideas. These ideas are so firmly embedded in your psyche that they may define who you think you are. The effect of honorable self-reflection is that you may have to admit that your worldview is at least partially false. This is asking a lot from any of us.

There is a reason I have structured this book the way I have. The previous chapters have not been easy reading. I have asked you to step through a series of concepts, each of which leads you to more information to reflect and build upon. This is done to layout a logical foundation which is one of the main precursors to wisdom. Wisdom can be defined as the "Capacity of judging rightly in matters relating to life and conduct; soundness of judgment in the choice of means and ends." These characteristics cannot be embedded into the fabric and DNA of our being, without a clear and concise regimen that allows us to determine truth; especially when distinguishing truth from honest but oversimplified ideas of faith (faith is fine, just remember to call it that and not ask for proof) in the absence of verifiable proof or, at the very least, a firm line of plausible logic.

As we have seen absolute truth is very difficult to verify; however, strong chains of logic by the use and grounding found in the five pillars of knowledge can assure us that we have done the best we can and give us an honorable path that leads most likely to positive results. The reason for this chapter is to pry a wedge between believing in what is the most probable truth and what the ego falsely tells us the truth is. Mastering the ego is hard work, but work that cannot begin before we come face to face with the fact that we have soared to perilous heights, and like Icarus we are doomed to fall when the false message begins to melt.

So, what is the good news? It is that the ego plays a major role in the struggles of humanity throughout all cultures and all times. Every culture has its stories of runaway egos, every religion, and spiritual practice has admissions and prohibitions regarding the overactive ego. We are not alone in the struggle. For example, Zen teachings equate the ego with fear and say this on the subject: "Some fear is understandable, such as when we realize we must face a spiritual death to progress on our path. Although we may long to reach higher levels of consciousness, we aren't always so keen to let go of the habits and crutches that have propped up our current level of awareness." As the Sufi poet Rumi once said, "No one will find his way to the Court of Magnificence until he is annihilated."

Islam says, "(75:2, Asad) At this stage, we have become more aware of our ego, but we are still caught by it. We are in the grip of something that is not our best self, but we still let ourselves act badly."

The Bible says, "Proverbs 13: The fear of the Lord is hatred of evil. Pride, Ego, and Arrogance and the way of evil, and perverted speech I hate."

The Upanishads say, "The ego is known in Sanskrit as *aham-kara*, which means of the form of 'I am' or the 'self'. The ego-self is different from the ego mentioned in the Samkhya philosophy, which is but an aspect or principle (*tattva*) of nature (*Prakriti*). The ego-self is what an individual is in his or her waking state. It is the usurper of the throne of the soul. It pretends to be the real self, whereas, in reality, it is but a shadow."

A Taoist view: "One thing basic to the Taoist belief is a re-definition of 'self' or 'ego'. Taoists believe that the way we try to stand outside ourselves in the attempt of self-observation is the source of most, if not all, of our unhappiness and loneliness, simply because we observe. As such, we must see our 'self' as separate from other 'selves'. This creates many unnecessary and troublesome illusions, and is based on an untrue assumption: that organisms are specifically exclusive."

This was a quick review highlighting just five observations concerning the ego and its dangers. There should be no doubt about the concepts of the ego in human history. The warning signs are everywhere.

I should spend some time examining the idea that the 'ego' being an honorable traveler is not an all or nothing condition. I know persons who I would consider having overactive egos. Aside from the negative dogma that they have inculcated into their worldview, they are good and decent people. They hold down jobs, own homes, have children, honor their chosen faiths, and do good acts for their fellow man. These people range from average citizens to exceptional human beings. However, living a good life and having an overactive ego is mutually exclusive. I can't help but detect how parts of their ego-driven personality rob them of a chance to live a fuller life, encompassing a broader range of positive experiences. This does not detract from all the good deeds and practices that are woven into the complete fabric of their lives. It is wise to view the whole person before judging them. We all know life is a struggle filled with challenges that can swamp the stoutest of boats. What then should be our course? I do not have all the answers, but I do have some suggestions. Practice self-discipline, cultivate humility, strive for wisdom, be open and flexible when it is difficult. Be brutally honest with yourself, open yourself to the critiques of others, and trust in your own honest judgment, and above all don't lie to yourself.

WISDOM

History teaches us that men and nations behave wisely once they have exhausted all other alternatives.

—Abba Eban (1915–2002)

Only by wisdom does humankind save itself from ultimate obliteration.

—Bob Alba (1945–present).

WE SEEK TO DO WHAT SATISFIES US NOW AND AVOID THE long term as wisdom might admonish. Expediency is often the currency of action rather than sagacious deliberation and careful analysis of all the facts we can gather before moving on. Add this to our preconceived (called confirmation bias) ideas and, often, erroneous concepts; this is surely a train wreck waiting to happen. It is true that over-analysis leads to paralysis, the lack of appropriate analysis can just as easily lead to catastrophe. Such was the case after 9/11. The United States conducted a military operation in a country which, it turned out, had nothing to do with 9/11. As of October 2010, 109,032 lives were lost because of that war. No weapons of mass destruction were ever found, and no link was ever documented or established regarding 9/11. The Congressional Budget Office reports that, as of 2017, the wars in Iraq and Afghanistan cost 2.4 trillion dollars.

This is not to question the decisions to go to war, but given the cost in lives and treasure, we cannot help to ask if a different path had been chosen, would it follow the track of wisdom and patience rather than political expedience and a rush to judgment. What a difference it could have made. History will be the final arbiter, but one thing is for sure, our actions, and decades of questionable Middle-Eastern policy, played an indelible role in fermenting the ascendancy of distrust and antagonism toward us in that part of the world. Our hands are not clean in this matter.

In the interest of full disclosure, I was a Marine who fought in Vietnam in 1965-67. This military action caused, by one estimate, 3,095,000 deaths and cost between 350 -900 billion dollars. While I was there, I took the time to educate myself on the history of Vietnam. In the end, I was convinced that it was an invasion of the South by the North, but today I seriously question the integrity of our politician's rationale for involving us the way it did.

History, by its nature, is never clear or clean. It's a messy affair, and we should always remember that countries, as people, always act in their assumed best interests. Their morals and ethics are the same on each side, which is to say questionable at best.

Individuals, in wise the decision-making process, are much the same as nations. Here is one definition of the quality of wisdom:

"The soundness of an action or decision with regard to the application of experience, knowledge, (evidence: my insertion) and good judgment." Let me provide an example: It seems to me that what we learned about Vietnam vis-à-vis the French Indo-china war, and the invasion of Afghanistan by the Russians these experiences should have enlightened us of the dangerous situation we were putting ourselves and thus tempered our actions. We did not choose wisdom and the result is plainly visible on the headline to this very day.

Let us not be naive, geopolitics is anything but simple. The roots of history may lie thousands of years in the past, intricately woven and tangled by events and personalities. We can only apply wisdom using the scrupulous investigation of history and its outcomes, a clear understanding of the present, and imagination of what our future actions might bring. These choices will be made at the zenith of the decision tree, far from the individual citizen. Therefore, we must choose our leaders wisely.

The smallest unit of our society (the individual) should aspire to wisdom. A diagram of this decision hierarchy tree is like an inverted pyramid and starts at the bottom with us. As we move up in wider and wider levels of responsibility and authority for more global decisions, we encounter groups of decision-makers like neighborhood groups, city councils, county, the state, and the federal government. If each unit in the hierarchy is not imbued with the ability to make wise decisions, then what can be the outcome? It can only be a dysfunctional condition which is what we face today.

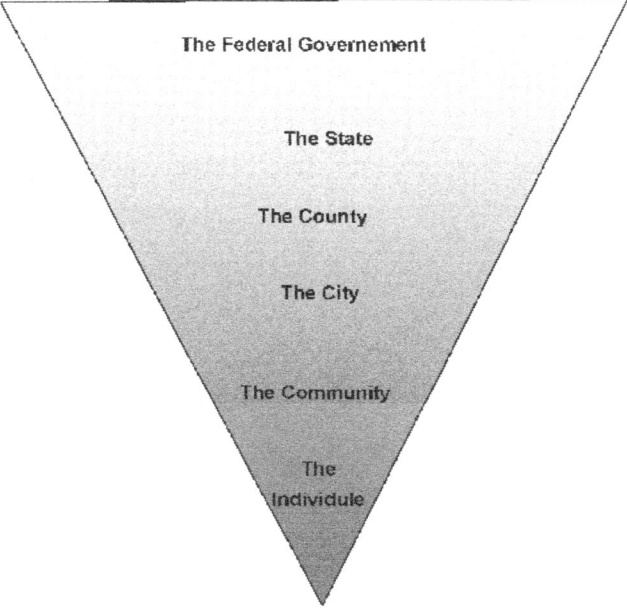

The logical question is, "why isn't wise thinking and acting taught at every educational institute if it is so important?" My guess is that if a parent doesn't teach these concepts to their children, they don't insist that it be part of a child's education from grade school onward. The universities and colleges don't make it a mandatory subject, why not? It's hard to believe that our entire social system is asleep at the grassroots level.

Maybe we all think it is taught in our places of worship. I would like to believe this, but I don't think it is true. I think a lot of time is spent on teaching to "being good," following the precept of whatever religion or spiritual practice we follow, but wisdom, critical thinking is not taught. It's not good enough to be a "moral" person and go to heaven or attain nirvana.

Wisdom is a practical choice and not a self-imbedded spiritual one. Wisdom is: "the soundness of an action or decision with regard to the application of experience, knowledge, and good judgment" (Pigliucci 2020). Wisdom may lead to a good choice, but this is not the essence of wisdom itself only a probable outcome if applied.

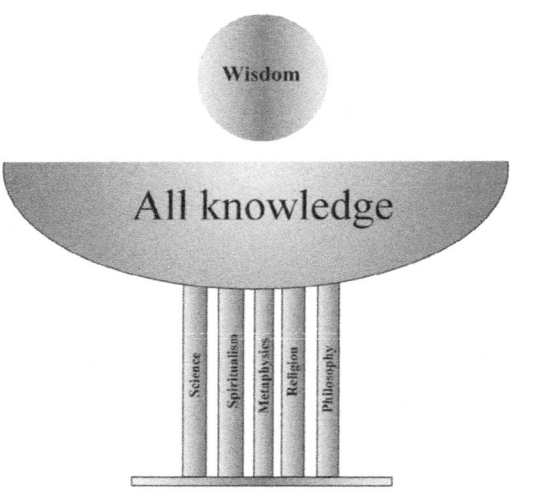

My objective in writing this book, in the format that I did, was to provide a layer of logical foundation, overlapping with separate ideas or concepts in which wisdom is applied to the previous layers. By way of the illustration below, let me see if I can be clear. The cup is represented by a base of cognition, the five stems represent science, spirituality, metaphysics, religion, and philosophy. Inside each stem, the various branches or sub-disciplines are contained, for example, the first stem contains all the forms of science from astrophysics to zoology. The stem representing spiritualism contains all the subsets of such persuasions, religion contains Christianity, Islam, etc. and so on. Thus, all human knowledge is represented. The bowl of the cup is where all these elements of knowledge are mixed. To drink from this cup is to take in all the knowledge. Notice that wisdom lies outside and above the cup. This is because, without wisdom, knowledge is not enough. Imagine then that you would need to drink from the cup of knowledge in a comprehensive manner, and then partake of wisdom to bring it all together.

In this way, you not only gain the knowledge to understand but the wisdom to execute what you learned in such a way that leads to the best possible outcome. This makes logical sense and leads to a sound strategy that can make a person well-balanced.

What practical effects does this hold on our country? Let's look at some of our most important institutions: Law and Order, Education, Health Care, Military, Human Services, and our Economy.

Law and Order

"Historic rates of fatal police shootings in Europe suggest that American police in 2014 were 18 times more lethal than Danish police, and 100 times more deadly than Finnish police, additionally, U.S. law enforcement killed significantly more frequently than police in France, Sweden, and other European countries."

"The U.S. incarcerates 716 people for every 100,000 residents, more than any other country. In fact, our rate of incarceration is more than five times higher than most of the countries in the world. Even though our level of crime is comparable to those of other stable, internally secure, industrialized nations, the United States shows an incarceration rate far higher than any other country."

"Nearly all the countries with relatively high incarceration rates share the experience of recent large-scale internal conflict. The United States, which enjoyed a long history of political stability and hasn't had a civil war in almost a century and a half, tops the list."

"Though only 5 percent of the world's population lives in the United States, it is home to 25 percent of the world's prison population. ... Not only does the current overpopulated, underfunded system hurt those incarcerated, it also digs deeper into the pockets of taxpaying Americans." (Lee 2015)

Education

"The U.S. education system is mediocre compared to the rest of the world, according to an international ranking of OECD countries. The NFI-ODCE, short for Fund Index-Open-End Diversified Core Equity, is the first of the NCREIF Fund database products and is an index of investment returns reporting on both a historical and current basis, the results of 33 open-end commingled funds pursuing a core investment strategy, some of which exhibit performance histories dating back to the 1970s. The NFI-ODCE Index is capitalization-weighted and has reported gross of fees. Measurement is time-weighted. NCREIF will calculate the overall aggregated Index return."

"More than half a million 15-year-olds around the world took the program for International Student Assessment in 2012. The test, which is administered every three years and focuses largely on math, but includes minor sections in science and reading, is often used as a snapshot of the global state of education. The results, published today, show the U.S. trailing behind educational powerhouses like Korea and Finland."

"Not much changed since 2000 when the U.S. scored along with the OECD average in every subject. This year, the U.S. scores below average in math and ranks 17th among the 34 OECD countries. It scores close to the OECD average in science and reading and ranks 21st in science and 17th in reading."

Fifteen percent of the American score variation is explained by socioeconomic differences between students. Less than 10 percent of score variation in Finland, Hong Kong, Japan, and Norway is due to socioeconomic differences. The U.S. also suffers from a lower than the average number of 'resilient students', which PISA defines as 'students who are among the 25 percent most socio-economically disadvantaged students but perform much better than would be predicted by their socioeconomic class'. On average, seven percent of students are considered resilient. Thirteen percent of students in Korea, Hong Kong, Macao-China, Shanghai-China, Singapore, and Vietnam are 'resilient'. (Ryan 2013)

Health Care

"In 2015, the United States spent almost three times more on healthcare as compared to other countries with comparable incomes, according to data from the Organization for Economic Cooperation and Development, also known as the OECD, a group of 35 countries, the majority of which boast of advanced economies and work to promote economic development. And, despite spending more, the results don't necessarily yield better health. Both Italy and Britain, for example, spent at least $5,000 less per person than the United States on healthcare, and yet the population of each of those countries exhibits a higher life expectancy at birth than the United States.

Experts explain that there are two underlying reasons why the United States spends so much on healthcare. It uses expensive medical technology and the prices for healthcare services and goods are higher than in other countries. As a result, the United States spends more on healthcare than any other country, including those belonging to the OECD.

The U.S. spends more money, but we definitely have worse health outcomes," said David Squires, president of the Commonwealth Fund, a private foundation based in New York which carries out independent research on healthcare issues. "It doesn't appear people in the U.S. use more healthcare in general. We go to the doctor less often than people in other countries and get hospitalized less, so it's not like we are making greater use, but we are paying more for the things we do use. (Etehad and Kim 2017)

Military

Global defense spending has increased for the first time since 2011, according to the latest report by the Stockholm International Peace Research Institute (SIPRI). In total, countries around the world splurged $1.686 trillion on arms in 2016, a 0.4 percent increase from 2015.

The United States remained at the top of the military spending league last year with $611 billion. 36 percent of the global total, and over three times the amount spent by second-placed China. Russia upped its outlay by 5.9 percent to $69.2 billion, third overall, according to the Swedish think tank.

Saudi Arabia was the world's third-largest military spender in 2015, and this year it dropped to the fourth position despite its considerable role in the conflict across its border in Yemen. Tensions with Russia have fueled military spending in Western Europe with overall spending growing 2.4 percent. Italy had the most notable increase in the region with its defense spending rising 11 percent to just under $28 billion. (Stockholm International Peace Research Institute 2020)

Human Services

In 2018, 88.9 percent of U.S. households were food secure throughout the year. The remaining 11.1 percent of households were food insecure at least some time during the year, including 4.3 percent (5.6 million households) that had very low food security.

Food insecurity was lower in 2018 than 2017 (11.8 percent). Food insecurity increased from 10.5 percent in 2000 to nearly 12 percent in 2004, declined to 11 percent in 2005–07, then increased to 14.6 in 2008. Food insecurity peaked at 14.9 percent in 2011 and has declined since.

In 2018, 35.3 percent of households with incomes below the Federal poverty line were food insecure. Food-insecure households include those with low food security and very low food security. Rates of food insecurity were substantially higher than the national average for single-parent households, and for Black and Hispanic households. Food insecurity was more common in large cities and rural areas than in suburban areas.

Parents often shield children from experiencing food insecurity, particularly very low food security, even when the parents themselves are food insecure. In 2018, 13.9 percent of households with children were food insecure. In about half of those food-insecure households with children, only the adults experienced food insecurity. But in 7.1 percent of households with children, both children and adults were food insecure sometime during the year. In 0.6 percent of U.S. households with children (220,000 households) both children and adults experienced instances of very low food security.

Food insecurity rates differ across States due to both the characteristics of their populations and to State-level policies and economic conditions. The estimated prevalence of food insecurity during 2016–18 ranged from 7.8 percent in New Hampshire to 16.8 percent in New Mexico. (Data for 2016–18 were combined to provide more reliable statistics at the State level.)

Federal expenditures for USDA's 15 food and nutrition assistance programs totaled $96.1 billion in fiscal 2018, or 3 percent less than the previous fiscal year. This was almost 12 percent less than the historical high of $109.2 billion set in fiscal 2013. Expenditures decreased by 5 percent for the Supplemental Nutrition Assistance Program (SNAP) and by 6 percent for the Special Supplemental Nutrition Program for Women, Infants, and Children (WIC) in fiscal 2018. Expenditures for the National School Lunch Program, the School Breakfast Program, and the Child and Adult Care Food Program, remained about the same.

In fiscal 2017, children accounted for 43.4 percent of all SNAP participants, slightly lower than in fiscal 2016 (44.1 percent). Children younger than five made up 13.4 percent of participants in fiscal 2016, while school-age children made up 30.0 percent. Adults age 18–59 represented 43.4 percent of SNAP participants in fiscal 2017, compared with 44.1 percent in fiscal 2016. Adults age 60 and older's share of the SNAP caseload grew from 11.8 percent in fiscal 2016 to 13.1 percent in fiscal 2017.

In fiscal 2018, SNAP served an average of 40.3 million people per month, or 12.3 percent of Americans. The percent of residents receiving SNAP benefits ranged from 21.8 percent in New Mexico to 5.1 percent in Wyoming. In fiscal 2018, Utah, New Hampshire, North Dakota, Kansas, Minnesota, and Colorado were the other States besides Wyoming with 8 percent or less of their populations receiving SNAP benefits. (US Department of Agriculture 2019)

Economy

President Donald Trump regularly and proudly takes credit for the US economy's strong performance. With rapid growth in the second quarter, the stock market strong, the unemployment rate back below 4 per cent and the midterm elections looming, his rhetoric and that of his supporters will probably escalate in the coming months. In fact, the approval the US president enjoys is boosted more by the strong economy, than the other way around. This conclusion will only be reinforced if Mr. Trump's current steps towards a trade war retard US economic performance, as is increasingly feared. A variety of observations are pertinent. First, history suggests that presidential popularity rises with declining unemployment. It is reasonable to suppose that, if unemployment were at its long-term level of 5.5 per cent, instead of its current 3.9 per cent, Mr. Trump's approval rate would fall lower than its already anemic level. As it is, his approval ratings are worse than those of any first-term president with an unemployment rate under 5 per cent. Second, such acceleration of growth as we have observed is well within the normal range of growth forecast errors. Before the 2016 election, when the Trump presidency was not anticipated, consensus forecasts for the US economy were 2.2 per cent for 2017, and 2.1 per cent for 2018. The actual outcome in 2017 of 2.2 per cent and the consensus forecast of 2.8 per cent for 2018 do not represent a statistically significant fluctuation from the mean. Third, it appears that growth has accelerated and exceeded expectations more outside the US than within the country, suggesting that whatever is driving America's growth is a global factor, rather than something for which US policy can take credit. For 2017, the country's growth exceeded expectations by less than for the world as a whole, or for China, Europe or Japan. For 2017 and 2018 taken together, US growth looks likely to exceed expectations by less than world growth. Fourth, market evidence calls into question the idea that the US has become a highly attractive place to invest because of Mr. Trump's policies. Net foreign direct investment in the US in the first quarter of 2018 was down nearly two-thirds against the first quarter of 2016. Goldman Sachs analysts have demonstrated that US companies which do more business abroad have outperformed those that are more domestically focused. And there is the basic observation that before trade war fears took hold, the dollar had declined during the Trump presidency. Fifth, the underlying reason why the US economy is strong right now is that it has been possible to run a very taut economy with unemployment below 4 per cent and not face significant inflationary pressures. No one is quite sure why this should be. It is probable that some combination of globalization, technology, and the reduction of employee power as unions have weakened have changed the inflation process. It is hard to see why Mr. Trump deserves credit for these structural changes, which have been happening for a long time. Sixth, there is what Ben Bernanke, the former Federal Reserve chairman, has labelled the 'Wile E Coyote' issue, after the accident-prone cartoon character. It may well be that an element of current success that can be attributed to Trump administration policy is borrowing prosperity from the future. This is most obvious in the case of the soyabean exports that were accelerated to avoid tariffs, but it is fairly ubiquitous. Increasing fiscal stimulus is like a drug with tolerance effects — to keep growth constant, deficits have to keep getting larger. Some combination of gathering foreign storm clouds, the end of growing fiscal stimulus and the delayed effect of tightening monetary policies may converge to slow or end the expansion. The choices this administration are making invite foreign retaliation against US exporters and use up fiscal capacity even as the economy is growing rapidly. Because of this, and because there is limited room for monetary policy, the country will not be in a position to respond strongly if a downturn comes, therefore, why we should avoid pulling demand forward. All the more reason. (Summers 2018)

I know that some of you were mentally creating counterarguments even before you finished reading this. Such is the human condition. But no worry, if things were different, we wouldn't be where we are today. I believe that there are enough of you out there to pay attention and try today to begin your journey toward acquiring wisdom, and for that I am grateful.

REALITY

*What our eyes behold may well be the text of life but
one's meditations on the text and the disclosures of these
meditations are no less a part of the structure of reality.*

—Wallace Stevens (1879–1955)

ATTEMPTING TO UNDERSTAND WHAT REALITY IS, IS ONE
of the endpoints of this book. All-be-it we are not there yet, and we
still have important and pertinent ground to cover before we arrive.

Reality can be defined in a way that links it to worldviews or parts
of them (conceptual frameworks). Reality is the totality of all things,
structures, events (past and present), phenomena, whether observable
or not. It is what a worldview (whether it be based on individual or
shared human experience) ultimately attempts to describe or map.

There are many viewpoints on this with anti-reality pundits
standing their ground claiming there is no objective universal reality

and there are some interesting arguments to back this point of view as well.

Let's review what early thinker thought on the subject.

There is more than one classification of reality. The reality that is thought of as physical existence as opposed to that which is only imaginary. It is the name given to physical existence, but the word is also used to speak of parts of reality that include the cognitive idea of an individual "reality" for example psychological and situational reality, or fictional reality.

The term is also used to refer to the ontological perspective (Ontology is the philosophical study of being). More broadly, ontology studies concepts that exactly relate to being, especially concerned with coming into existence and reality, as well as the basic categories of being and their relations to the status of things, indicating their existence, but this is only the idea of giving names to smaller "realities," and seems vague and academic without the idea of physical existence as the first "reality," of which others are smaller parts.

Philosophical questions about the nature of reality or existence or being are considered under the rubric of ontology, which is a major branch of metaphysics in the Western philosophical discourse. Ontological questions also feature diverse branches of philosophy, including the philosophy of science, philosophy of religion, philosophy of mathematics, and philosophical logic. These include questions about whether only physical objects are real (i.e., Physicalism), whether reality is fundamentally immaterial (e.g., Idealism), whether hypothetical unobservable entities posited by scientific theories exist, whether God exists, whether numbers and other abstract objects exist, and whether other possible worlds exist. Certain ideas from physics, philosophy, sociology, literary criticism, and other fields shape various theories of reality. One such belief is that there obviously and literally is no reality beyond the perceptions or beliefs that each of us has about reality. Such attitudes are summarized in the popular statement, "Perception is reality" or "Life is how you perceive reality" or "the reality is what you can get away with" (Robert Anton Wilson), and they indicate that anti-realism is the view that there is no objective reality, whether acknowledged clearly or not.

Many of the concepts of science and philosophy are often defined culturally and socially. This idea was elaborated on by Thomas Kuhn in his book *The Structure of Scientific Revolutions* (1962). *The Social Construction of Reality*, a book about the sociology of knowledge, written by Peter L. Berger and Thomas Luckmann, was published in 1966. It explains how knowledge is acquired and used for the comprehension of reality. Out of all the realities, the reality of everyday life is the most important one since our consciousness requires us to be aware and attentive to the experience of everyday life.

The nature of being is a perennial topic in metaphysics. For, instance Parmenides taught reality was a single unchanging Being, whereas Heraclitus wrote that all things flow. The 20th-century philosopher, Heidegger, thought that previous philosophers had lost sight of the question of Being (qua Being), in favor of the questions of beings (existing things), and therefore, a return to the Parmenidean approach was needed. An ontological catalog is an attempt to list the fundamental constituents of reality. Whether existence is a predicate has been discussed since the early modern period, not least in relation to the ontological argument for the existence of God. (Wikipedia 2020)

The proposition that existence precedes essence : *l'existence précède l'essence*) is a central claim of existentialism, which reverses the traditional philosophical view that the essence (the nature) of a thing is more fundamental and immutable than its existence (the mere fact of its being).[1] To existentialists, human beings—through their consciousness—create their own values and determine a meaning for their life because the human being does not possess any inherent identity or value. That identity or value must be created by the individual. By posing the acts that constitute them, they make their existence more significant. (Wikipedia 2020)

This question of direct or naive realism, as opposed to indirect or representational realism, arises in the philosophy of perception and mind, out of the debate over the nature of conscious experience; the epistemological question is whether the world we see around us is the real world itself or an internal perceptual copy of that world generated by the neural processes in our brain. Naive realism is known as *direct* realism when developed to counter *indirect* or representational realism. This is also known as epistemological dualism, the philosophical position that our conscious experience is not of the real world itself but an internal representation, a miniature virtual-reality replica of the world.

The status of abstract entities, particularly numbers, is a topic of discussion in mathematics.

In the philosophy of mathematics, the best-known form of realism of numbers is Platonic realism, which grants them abstract, immaterial existence. Other forms of realism identify mathematics with the concrete physical universe. Anti-realist stances include formalism and fictionalism. Some approaches are selectively realistic about some mathematical objects but not others. Finitism rejects infinite quantities. Ultra-finitism accepts finite quantities up to a certain amount. Constructivism and intuitionism are realistic about objects that can be openly constructed but reject the use of the principle of the excluded middle to prove existence by *reductio ad absurdum*.

The traditional debate has focused on whether an abstract (immaterial, intelligible) realm of numbers has existed in addition to the physical (sensible, concrete) world. A recent development is the mathematical universe hypothesis, the theory that only a mathematical world exists, with the finite, physical world being an illusion within it. An extreme form of realism about mathematics is the mathematical multiverse ("While the idea of a multiverse sounds like something straight out of science fiction, physicists have advanced three distinct arguments.")

The first involves the Big Bang, the cataclysmic event that brought the universe into existence some 13.8 billion years ago. The Big Bang is thought to have been triggered by a random fluctuation in what physicists call the quantum foam, a maelstrom of virtual particles that pop into and out of existence. But while some physicists believe this blip and the ensuing "inflation" of the universe constitute a unique event, others say there could have been many such events— leading to multiple universes.

The second argument for the existence of a multiverse arises from string theory, which holds that matter is ultimately composed not of particles but of unimaginably small, vibrating strings or loops of energy. Physicists once hoped that string theory might afford a "theory of everything"—that is, a system of equations that explains why our universe has the exact properties that it does. For example, why is the mass of a proton 1836.15 times greater than that of the electron? No one has a good explanation.

But instead of a single solution to this and other fundamental scientific questions, string theory's equations seem to have a staggering number of possible solutions (perhaps as many as 10^{500}—that's a one followed by 500 zeros). Some string theorists argue that each of these solutions describes a different universe, each with its own physical properties.

The third argument for the multiverse comes from quantum theory. Although it's been around for more than a century now and has proven to be extremely successful at describing the nature of matter on the smallest scale, quantum theory leads to a number of existential possibilities that defy common sense. In what's known as the "many worlds" interpretation of quantum theory, which got its start in the 1950s and has recently seen renewed interest, the universe essentially splits in two each time there's a so-called quantum event.

In the upside-down world of quantum theory, for instance, a radioactive particle decays and doesn't decay during any given period of time—and each result plays out in a separate universe. With such quantum events happening more or less continuously, the argument goes, the number of universes keeps increasing.) (Falk 2018) hypothesis advanced by Max Tegmark. Tegmark's sole postulate is this: *All structures that exist mathematically, also exist materially.* That is, in this sense, "in those (worlds) complex enough to contain self-aware sub-structures (they) will subjectively perceive themselves as existing in a 'real' world." The hypothesis suggests that worlds corresponding to different sets of initial conditions, physical constants, or altogether different equations should be considered real. The theory can be considered a form of Platonism in which it posits the existence of mathematical entities but can also be considered a mathematical monism in that it denies anything exists except mathematical objects.

The **problem of universals** is an ancient question from metaphysics which has inspired a range of philosophical topics and disputes. Should the properties an object has in common with other objects, such as color and shape, be considered to exist beyond those objects? And if a property exists separately from objects, what is the nature of that existence?[1]

The problem of universals relates to various inquiries closely related to metaphysics, logic, and epistemology, as far back as Plato and Aristotle, in efforts to define the mental connections a human makes when they understand a property such as shape or color to be the same in nonidentical objects.

Universals are qualities or relations found in two or more entities.[3] As an example, if all cup holders are *circular* in some way, *circularity* may be considered a universal property of cup holders.[4] Further, if two daughters can be considered *female offspring of Frank*, the qualities of being *female*, *offspring*, and *of Frank*, are universal properties of the two daughters. Many properties can be universal: being human, red, male or female, liquid or solid, big or small, etc."

"A traditional realist position in ontology is that time and space have an existence apart from the human mind. Idealists deny or doubt the existence of objects independent of the mind. Some anti-realists whose ontological position is that objects outside the mind do exist, nevertheless, doubt the independent existence of time and space.

Kant, in the *Critique of Pure Reason*, described time as an a priori notion, together with other a priori notions such as space, which allows us to comprehend sense-experience. Kant denies that either space or time are substances, entities in themselves, or learned by experience; he rather holds that both are elements of a systematic framework that we used to structure our experience. Spatial measurements are used to quantify how far apart objects are, and temporal measurements are used to quantitatively compare the interval between (or duration of) events. Although space and time are held to be transcendentally ideal in this sense, they are also empirically real, that is, not mere illusions.

Idealist writers such as J. M. E. McTaggart, in *The Unreality of Time*, have argued that time is an illusion. Along with differing about the reality of time as a whole, metaphysical theories of time can differ in their ascription of reality to the past, present, and future separately as well.

"The term 'possible world' goes back to Leibniz's theory of possible worlds, used to analyze necessity, possibility, and similar modal notions. Modal realism is the view, notably propounded by David Kellogg Lewis, that all possible worlds are as real as the actual world. In short, the actual world is regarded as merely one among an infinite set of logically possible worlds, some nearer to the actual world and some more remote. Other theorists may use the 'possible world' framework to express and explore problems without committing to it ontologically. Possible world theory is related to athletic logic: a proposition is necessary if it is true in all possible worlds, and possible if it is true in at least one. The many-worlds interpretation of quantum mechanics is a similar idea in science."

The philosophical implications of a physical TOE (The Theory of Everything) are frequently debated. For example, if philosophical physicalism is true, a physical TOE will coincide with a philosophical theory of everything. The system-building style of metaphysics attempts to answer all the important questions in a coherent way, providing a complete picture of the world. Plato and Aristotle could be said to be early examples of comprehensive systems. In the early modern period (seventeenth and eighteenth centuries), the system-building scope of philosophy is often linked to the rationalist method of philosophy, which is the technique of deducing the nature of the world with pure a priori reason. Examples include Leibniz's monadology, Descartes's dualism, Spinoza's monism, Hegel's absolute idealism, and Whitehead's process philosophy were later systems.

Other philosophers do not believe that its techniques can aim so high. Some scientists think a more mathematical approach is needed for the TOE. For instance, Stephen Hawking wrote in *A Brief History of Time* that even if we had a TOE, it would necessarily be a set of equations. He wrote, "What is it that breathes fire into the equations and makes a universe for them to describe?"

Reality is the sum or aggregate of all that is real or existent within a system, as opposed to that which is only imaginary. The term is also used to refer to the ontological status of things, indicating their existence.[1] In physical terms, reality is the totality of a system, known and unknown.[2] Philosophical questions about the nature of reality or existence or being are considered under the rubric of ontology, which is a major branch of metaphysics in the Western philosophical tradition. Ontological questions also feature in diverse branches of philosophy, including the philosophy of science, philosophy of religion, philosophy of mathematics, and philosophical logic. These include questions about whether only physical objects are real (i.e., Physicalism), whether reality is fundamentally immaterial (e.g., Idealism), whether hypothetical unobservable entities posited by scientific theories exist, whether God exists, whether numbers and other abstract objects exist, and whether possible worlds exist.

The debate over what the success of science involves centers on the real status of entities, which are not directly observable, discussed by scientific theories. Those who are scientific realists state that one can make reliable claims about these entities (viz., they have the same ontological status) as obvious observable entities, as opposed to instrumentalism. The most used and studied scientific theories today state the truth. (Wikipedia 2020)

On a much broader and more subjective level, private experiences, curiosity, inquiry, and the selectivity involved in a personal interpretation of events shape reality, as seen by one and only one individual, and hence, it is called phenomenological. While this form of reality might be common to others as well, it could at times also be so unique to oneself as to never be experienced or agreed upon by anyone else. Much of the kind of experience deemed spiritual occurs on this level of reality. Phenomenology is a philosophical method developed in the early years of the twentieth century by Edmund Husserl, and a circle of followers, at the universities of Göttingen and Munich in Germany. Subsequently, phenomenological themes were taken up by philosophers in France, the United States, and elsewhere, often in contexts far removed from Husserl's work. The word "phenomenology" comes from the Greek *phenomenon*, meaning "that which appears," and *logos, meaning "study.* "In Husserl's conception, phenomenology is primarily concerned with making the structures of consciousness, and the phenomena which appear in acts of consciousness, objects of systematic reflection and analysis. Such reflection was to take place from a highly modified 'first-person' viewpoint, studying phenomena not as they appear to 'my' consciousness, but to any consciousness whatsoever. Husserl believed that phenomenology could thus provide a firm basis for all human knowledge, including scientific knowledge, and could establish philosophy as 'rigorous science.'"

Husserl's conception of phenomenology has been criticized and developed not only by himself, but also by his student and assistant Martin Heidegger, by existentialists, such as Maurice Merleau-Ponty, Jean-Paul Sartre, and by other philosophers, such as Paul Ricoeur, Emmanuel Levinas, and Dietrich von Hildebrand.

In many philosophies, the conscious mind is considered to be a separate entity, existing in a parallel realm not described by physical law. Some people claim that this idea gains support from the description of the physical world provided by quantum mechanics. Parallels between quantum mechanics and mind/body dualism were first drawn by the founders of quantum mechanics.

The reason is that quantum mechanics requires interpretation before it describes the experience of an observer. While particles and fields are described by a wavefunction, the results of observations are described by classical information which tells you the result. The information about observations is not in the wavefunction, but is additional random data. The wavefunction gives only the probability of getting different outcomes, and it turns into a classical probability only during the act of measurement, when its magnitude squared gives a probability for different outcomes.[1]

The nature of observation has often been a point of contention in quantum mechanics,[2] because quantum mechanics describes the experiences of observers with different numbers than it uses to describe material objects. With the notable exceptions of Louis DeBroglie, Max von Laue, Erwin Schrödinger, and Albert Einstein,[3] who believed that quantum mechanics was a statistical approximation to a deeper reality which is deterministic, most of the founders of quantum mechanics believed that this problem is purely philosophical. Eugene Wigner went further, and explicitly identified it as a quantum version of the mind-body problem.

Classical mind/body problem

In classical mechanics the world is measurable, the measurements reveal the true state of the world, and the behavior is deterministic. Given the initial positions and momentum of a collection of the basic particles, the future of those particles can be predicted. When these assumptions are applied to an observer the conclusion is that with enough information about the present, the entire future behavior of the observer will be determined. This led many scientists to reject pre-scientific notions of dualism, and to identify the mind of the observer with the classical state of the observer's atoms.[5][6]

Yet even from a classical perspective many philosophers doubt that the material description of a hypothetical Newtonian observer is all that is necessary to understand internal experience. That is, they suggest that there may be a mind-body problem.[7][8][9] Even though the atoms of the brain are constantly replaced, the information gets copied into new atoms, and perception continues into the new brain. In certain thought experiments, this type of copying leads to strange outcomes. For example, Daniel Dennett talks about the situation where a conscious Newtonian observer is duplicated, by having a second system store all the information in the brain. Once the second system is built, the two systems make two separate observers which contain the same information. The two observers start out exactly the same and receive the same sensory input, but eventually diverge. The divergence could be due to randomness, or glitches, or because the sensory input is slightly different; the reason is not important. The important thing is that one observer has been copied into two systems, and in such a situation it is not clear to this observer into which of the copies their experiences will continue.

Dennett notes this by assuming that he himself is copied. Before the copies diverge, there is no way for him to know which of the two copies he is. This bit of information becomes apparent to Dennett only after the two copies become different. He cannot know this information before the divergence, even if he is given full information about the material state of both copies.[10]

Transition to Quantum Mechanics

The introduction of quantum mechanics substantially changed the status of the observer and measurements. The measurement problem studies how a classical observer can exist in a quantum world. The quantum world describes superpositions of very different states, but our perception is that of "classical" states in the macroscopic world, that is, a comparatively small subset of the states allowed by the quantum-mechanical superposition principle, having only a few, but determinate and robust, properties, such as position, momentum, etc. The question of why and how our experience of a "classical" world emerges from quantum mechanics thus lies at the heart of the foundational problems of quantum theory.

The determinism and materialism of classical mechanics divorced or at least distanced science from many pre-scientific philosophies that held various dualist perspectives toward the mind. Some scientists (like Wigner) believe that quantum mechanics makes certain dualist ideas about the mind/body problem accept-able again within mainstream science, while others[11] think there is little to gain from science entertaining those possibilities further (as described in the criticism section below). http://settheory.net/quantum-mind-body-problem

The founders of quantum mechanics debated the role of the observer, and of them, Wolfgang Pauli and Werner Heisenberg believed that it was the observer that produced collapse. This point of view, which was never fully endorsed by Niels Bohr, was denounced as mystical and anti-scientific by Albert Einstein. Pauli accepted the term and described quantum mechanics as lucid mysticism.

Heisenberg and Bohr always described quantum mechanics in logical positivist terms. Bohr also took an active interest in the phil-osophical implications of quantum theories such as his complemen-tarity. He believed that quantum theory offers a complete description of nature, albeit one that is simply ill-suited for everyday experiences, which are better described by classical mechanics and probability. Bohr never specified a demarcation line above which objects cease to be quantum and become classical. He believed that it was not a question of physics, but one of philosophy.

Eugene Wigner reformulated the "Schrödinger's cat" thought experiment as "Wigner's friend," and proposed that the conscious-ness of an observer is the demarcation line which precipitates the collapse of the wave function, independent of any realist interpre-tation. Commonly known as "consciousness causes collapse," this interpretation of quantum mechanics states that observation by a conscious observer is what makes the wave function collapse.

As you can see by now, the view of what is real and what is not, and where and when does it exist, is not straight forward and is encompassed in several practical, philosophic, and scientific domains. What is important to us is that it is not monolithic or set in stone. This leaves the door open to a number of non-traditional viewpoints. This is extremely important because when taken together with all the other subjects presented so far, we can be prepared to launch into the darkness of the unknown from a firm platform of reason into realms that may be completely different from our current worldview. Therefore, I have asked you to consider that there may be more than you think you know, and there are rational thoughts and presidency behind these novel concepts.

At this point, it appears as though we are ready to ask some general questions. The title of the book is *An Honorable Journey: In Search of the Truth*. I have labeled it a journey because that is what this process is. But more than that, it is based on the honest quest to build from the solid foundation of knowledge, in the five domains of human observation and study. This was built by trying to understand the very footing upon each rest, to provide a solid footing to support the logical magic of truth. Domains or kingdoms, as I have called them, attempt to neutralize or demean each other. They look at precepts and concepts from different perspectives, but generally form a web of mutual support and cooperation leading to a better idea of what we can call the truth. All paths head in the direction of something we can all believe in, even when our starting point is far afield from our neighbor.

What is real is universal, but how you perceive it is not. But only in the details, just like the world's thousands of different languages can be translated into accurate and concrete meaning, understandable to all, so it is with the truth. We all long to know who we are and what life means. This search has been going on since we become sentient. I believe we are all excruciatingly, slowly moving together to find a common home of belief.

We already have more in common than not at the basic level. By far, those differences have had to do with the journey each of us, along with our ancestors, took to where we are today, mostly the difference is in details, artifacts of culture, devices used for walking us through the eons of social travel. These are just things we picked up along the way to make it easier to deal with our common road-blocks for survival.

Since we each started our journey from so many parts of the world, over thousands and thousands of years old, it is no wonder we developed such diverse cultures and beliefs. History has molded us to deal with every triumph and defeat and to keep us moving toward the future. It is my belief that all our paths are converging, and even though the road ahead is still very long, we will one day meet with one universal truth. As you can see there are many ways to conceive reality. It is a quality that is based on our perspective. I believe that, at the widest, the most inclusive viewpoint of reality encompasses a way of looking at the world that will dazzle us with its simplicity. From all our knowledge, and that yet to be discovered, reality will converge at one point which is the basic nature of what we call existence.

CONCEPTUAL NAVIGATION

I may not have gone where I intended to go,
but I think I have ended up where I needed to be.

—Douglas Adams

YOU MAY NOTICE THAT I BUILT-IN "WAYPOINTS" ALONG with the progression of this book. This is because I understood that the book had to be a logical unfolding of ideas or concepts, laid out in a particular order, like steps along a mountain path, in order for you to arrive at my intended coordinates. This is my attempt at conceptual navigation, a road map of sorts leading to a deep understanding of a conceptually difficult way of looking at life.

If I had introduced the endpoint of the book at the beginning, I believe you would not have had the foundation needed to fully appreciate the concepts I am going to propose. So, let's take one more glance into the rearview mirror to make sure we are still on the appropriate path. By the time you stumble on this book, you will probably have created a worldview based on the fundamental knowledge of how you perceive how the world works. You used your formal education, life experiences, instincts, and focus toward ideas about life that have been naturally fermenting in your mind for years. Our life experiences, and history, will form the basis of what we believe in. The roots of our worldview run deep; sometimes we may not even know how they came to be. This view of who we are started out on the blank page of the story of our life as you exited the womb and one by one the text was added to make as complete a narrative of your life as exists today.

This is not an autobiography; we are characters in the book, not the author. The honor of filling in the pages was left to the deft hand of fate. Sometimes we directed the action in the book but most of the time the story seemed to appear itself, as the winds of fortune and the tides within the empty pages carried us to unplanned locations. If you made it this far, after reading this book, note that I tried to highlight the tools in the form of character traits that you will need to forge ahead with a more defined and deliberate path.

What I offer is not totally novel, although some of the ideas are. But depending on where you are on the path of experience and maturity, it will serve you well. This book is for those, no matter where they are in their journey, to go much further. I am not naive and give myself credit for being wise and being better suited than anyone else to serve as a guild. I only possess the knowledge and contemplation that seventy-four years have given me, for better or worse.

Truth

In any event, what is needed now are the traits we have reviewed so far. We need a firm grounding to understand the background of the concept of truth. We need to know that there are formal ways of identifying and justifying the truth. We need to understand that truth is not an opinion and it is not malleable; the truth is pure and subject to testing and careful scrutiny. Truth must be able to withstand any challenge. It is not arbitrary, and it is never based on faith. Its veracity is never vacuous and founded on questionable arguments, and it is always subject to defense by those who propose the subject to be true. Truth, always, must be subject to evidence and the evidence must be backed by scrupulous examination and verification. In the end, we must be our own final arbiters of what we believe to be true by using the formal anchors of those who come before us. However, we can never give in to the self-imposed mental and spiritual athletics of self-deceit.

Philosophy

Philosophy is the study of knowledge. This study defines what real knowledge is. The philosophical study is the framework by which we classify and define areas of knowledge. Its vast array of subfields lay the foundation to study how we come to hold truth as reliable. Philosophical tenets form the foundation for how we understand the knowledge and where and how it comes to us. Since knowledge leads to the foundation of what we believe in, we find that philosophical thinking provides a frame of reference from which to judge the quality of the knowledge we seek.

Evidence

Evidence illuminates and purifies truth. Truth without evidence cannot be verified. Those making assertions are responsible to lay out the evidence which supports their assertions. Human culture has developed a rule of evidence to confirm its veracity. These rules stand beside truth to confirm its claims.

In this case, we also note that belief is the antithesis of proof. David Hume in his, *An Inquiry Concerning Understanding,* stated, "A wise man proportions his belief to the evidence."

According to an article in the Sanford Encyclopedia of Philosophy, "As a general matter, the evidence seems to play a mediating role vis-à-vis and effort to arrive at an accurate picture of the world: we seek to believe what is true by means of holding beliefs that are well-supported by the evidence and seek to avoid believing what is false by mean of not holding beliefs which are not well-supported by the evidence."

Blanchard well summarizes the picture as follows, "Surely the only possible rule, one may say, is to believe what is true and disbelieve what is false. And, of course, that would be the rule if we were in a position to know what was true and what was false. The whole difficulty arises from the fact we do not and often cannot. What is to guide us?... The idea is to believe no more, but no less, than what the evidence warrants."

Another important issue in the discourse of evidence comes to focus when we arrive at the subject of the "burden of proof." Who is responsible to provide the proof through evidence? This task is held to be the responsibility of the person or body who makes an assertion and is asking others to believe the assertion. In modern times, this is an important point and it should be noted that the "party to be convinced" does not have the obligation to prove otherwise. However, this is not the same as not having the responsibility to rebut the asserter's evidence and proof.

Faith

There is one more important subject we must address before we leave the benefits of religion and spirituality. That is "faith versus fact." This is a passionately charged topic for most adherents since they believe their religion or spiritual worldview is a fact and is the only true viewpoint. While I realize that in the eyes of the believers this must be so, it creates amongst all traditions an unsolvable paradox. All religions at once cannot be the true religion or spiritual truth. This question can only return one other outcome and that is no religion or spiritual belief is fact or the true path. While religion and spirituality are immensely helpful, they are often mistaken in their assumption that only one truth is available. We must be flexible and tolerant.

At the same time, we ask those disposed toward religion and spirituality to be nondogmatic. We must also ask that those who are not disposed to belief, based on faith, be patient. Belief in faith is deeply embedded in the psyche and when we ask the religious believer for flexibility, it is essential that we respect their point of view. It is possible for a person to be open to other viewpoints without feeling like their views are being violated, and to understand that to be focused on truth as illuminated by a non-religious or spiritual worldview does not mean that their view does not need to be extinguished. Believing is a very personal issue and can be highly emotionally charged so, while not accepting a proposition as true, there is no need to disrespect it.

Science

Science relies on logical augments called theories. These theories are understood as a proposition of ideas about some subject which can be supported and verified in a way that they can stand the scrutiny of other peers in the field of study. The scientific method is used as a scaffolding to lay the groundwork and the supporting evidence.

The scientific method is an empirical method of knowledge acquisition that has characterized the development of natural science since, at least, the seventeenth century. It involves careful observation, which includes rigorous skepticism about what is observed, given that cognitive assumptions about how the world works influence how one interprets a precept. It involves formulating hypotheses, via deduction, based on such observations—experimental and measurement-based testing of deductions drawn from the hypotheses and refinement (or elimination) of the hypotheses based on the experimental findings.

As can be seen in the definition, science is based on factual truth to the extent that the theory and subsequent challenges can support a conclusion, and then also only as long as an opposing or expanded theory does not overtake and replace it. In this realm, there can be no room for pure faith.

Reality

It is from the above constituents that we build our reality in a way that leads us to the truth. Truth is reality, but the reality is decidedly malleable depending on how it is defined. For example, a person may hold that reality is based on their personal point of view. Unfortunately, if we evoke truth into the equation of reality it may not pass the test and maybe found not to be the truth.

Therefore, there is an unbreakable connection between reality and truth in the absolute sense.

There are circumstances where truth, in the scientific sense, is counterintuitive but has been verified by rigid mathematical verification and experiment. One such example is in the realm of QP, in an area that Einstein called the "spooky science at a distance." He was talking about a feature that QP calls "locality" of space. In this paradigm it is said that all space is "local," and one thing here cannot affect a thing there unless they can touch each other. But a phenomenon called "entanglement" can destroy locality. In essence, we can take an atom or other subatomic particles, and cause them to become entangled so that the spin or other property of a local particle can affect the same characteristic of another particle at the opposite side of the universe instantaneously. This has been done at shorter ranges here on Earth, and the phenomenon has been proven to be 100 percent true when extrapolated at any distance. Science does not know how this can be true and how it defies the locality rule, but it does.

Entanglement is true but it defies straight forward intuition. Here reality and truth support each other, but we don't know the mechanism of action (how it works).

In the next chapter, we will explore novel new concepts regarding the reality, and find them to be completely foreign, but just as viable as any other religious, spiritual, philosophical view and, in many ways, supported by science.

"HOW MUCH CAN HUMANS KNOW?"

The capability of human life is beyond our imagination.

What counts is the human capacity to investigate and transform our own mind and the world around us in a powerful and positive direction.

—Gelek Rinpoche

THIS COULD BE ONE OF THE MOST SIGNIFICANT CHAPters of the book. As you can see from the reading so far, this book is information-dense. The subjects, though varied and intimately related, must include some effort to help the reader navigate in a way that the whole book is made clear. Each chapter stands alone but is integrated into a cogent whole. The information presented may be too much to ask any reader to hold in their mind all at once.

Leapfrogging from one chapter to another, and stacking the information so that it makes sense can be challenging. Therefore, it is important for the reader to understand that it is vital to keep the information learned and integrated into memory so a full story can logically unfold.

The process is analogous to preparing a food dish. The outcome is unfamiliar to the person preparing the dish without knowing what they have to do before they start. In this example, the process is to blindly follow the instructions one is given. One can surmise, seeing the ingredients and the materials and equipment provided, that they are preparing food, but the end result is completely unknown as is the dish being prepared.

In the same manner, I assure you that you will not be able to guess what details the final chapter will reveal. What I can tell you is that the final chapter has some rather non-traditional perspectives. For this reason, I have carefully put together enough information that can support my conclusions. However, the conclusions will beg the question of how I know what I say is possible? That is a fair question.

This is why I need to support, using all the other chapters together, my premise. Still, we can ask how we know what we don't know? From years of study and contemplation, it became increasingly clear to me that a critical bit of information needed to be amassed and correlated to build a full spectrum narrative to support my thesis. As I reviewed the amount and scope of information needed, it became obvious that this would be a lifetime worth of knowledge. The natural question in my mind was if it is possible for one to accomplish this? Given my conclusion, I couldn't help but ask, is a human capable of acquiring this knowledge. Broadly, the question is how much humans can know? Experience, long ago, taught me that there is a wide chasm between knowledge and information. Let me give you an example. I know a person who collected and read a library of over three thousand books covering a considerable variety of subjects from ancient history, biology, anatomy, astronomy, and many more. This person processes a reasonable mastery of the collective subjects in his library. He worked for a well-known aerospace organization as a researcher and an un-degreed engineer. He held a variety of positions in more than a few countries. You might be thinking this guy is pretty smart. The definition of SMART is an acronym for five elements including specific, measurable, achievable, relevant, and time-based goals.

But curiously, this person, as smart as you might think his life is and has been, is a perpetual mess. Now, at an advanced age he still struggles to make steady progress in his rather tumultuous life. While I applaud him for all his legitimate accomplishments, I know that he lived a life far below his potential. The problem is that he has not been able to integrate and consistently master all the information he has gathered in his life. Thus, he lives on the fringe. In my opinion, he will not be able to master the tenets of this book. I sincerely hope I am wrong, but I honestly believe he will never travel an honorable journey.

So, by this example, you can see that it is possible to be smart and yet not possess the tools it takes to be an enlightened person who has true knowledge. This is an example of a person who has a lot of information but has not been able to integrate it with other critical human character traits of a higher realm.

Let's switch now and look at what science has to say about our human capacity to collect information and the correlation with what I call true knowledge. What a human can know, strongly corresponds to the brain's capacity to store information in the trillions of synapses each brain contains. Other factors are also important. What we can learn is limited by the amount of time we have to enter the information into our brain. We sleep about one-third of our life. Time is limited. New information is primarily blocked by about 30 percent of our lives as we sleep. In addition, in order to learn, we must be paying close attention and unfortunately, most of us have limited attention spans and these are further limited by our ability to pay attention to more than a few things at a time. Paying attention is the only way we can create new lasting memories and thus new information and knowledge. It follows that the more impoverished is our ability to pay optimal attention is, the less information we can store, create, memorize, and learn.

The order in which we gather information is also vital. The earlier we obtain the information, the stronger we capture it. Language is one of the things we learn first. This is why it is much easier for children to learn multiple languages than it is for adults. The older we get the more difficult it is to expand our usable information vault. Given these limitations, the human brain still has a prodigious capacity with its 100 billion neurons and 100 trillion synapses. This gives a storage capacity measured in petrobytes or millions of megabytes.

Compare this to the largest, most powerful supercomputers and the brain wins by miles.

"At the time of this writing, the fastest supercomputer in the world is the *Tianhe-2* in Guangzhou, China, and has a maximum processing speed of 54.902 petaflops. A petaflop is a quadrillion (one thousand trillion) floating-point calculations per second. This is a huge amount of calculations, and yet, that doesn't come close to the processing speed of the human brain. In contrast, our miraculous brains operate on the next higher order. Although it is impossible to precisely calculate, it is postulated that the human brain operates at 1 exaflop, which is equivalent to a quintillion, calculations per second." https://www.lesswrong.com/users/tehuti

For now, I will stay away from discussing how and why we lose memories. For our purposes, we can conclude that yes, the human brain has the capacity to store much more information than is needed for the author this book to arrive at its conclusions.

However, raw information is not enough to collectively call it usable knowledge any more than Google can use all its data, across thousands of subjects, to create usable integrated knowledge. A human is needed to take the information and make it something greater than itself.

It is believed that the major area of assembling individual bits of information together is in the frontal lobes of the brain. This is located behind the forehead. The brain collects these bits as memories from various locations of the brain and joins them together in the frontal lobes.

Remember, much is not known about how the brain functions, so, I have taken some liberties here for the sake of brevity and complete accuracy.

How does the conversion of raw information to knowledge take place?

"Linguists and cognitive psychologists, have used the concept of the schema (plural: schemata) to understand the interaction of key factors affecting the comprehension process. Simply put, schema theory states that all knowledge is organized into units. Within these units of knowledge, or schemata is stored information. A schema, then, is a generalized description or a conceptual system for understanding knowledge: how knowledge is represented and how it is used. According to this theory, schemata represent knowledge about concepts: objects and the relationships they have with other objects, situations, events, sequences of events, actions, and sequences of actions. A simple example is to think of your schema for a dog. Within that schema, you most likely have knowledge about dogs in general (bark, four legs, teeth, hair, tails) and probably information about specific dogs, such as collies (long hair, large, Lassie) or springer spaniels (English, docked tails, liver and white or black and white, Millie). You may also think of dogs within the greater context of animals and other living things; that is, dogs breathe, need food, and reproduce. Your knowledge of dogs might also include the fact that they are mammals and thus are warm-blooded and bear their young as opposed to laying eggs. Depending upon your personal experience, the knowledge of a dog as a pet (domesticated and loyal) or as an animal to fear (likely to bite or attack) may be a part of your schema.

And so, it goes with the development of a schema. Each new experience incorporates more information into one's schema. What does all this have to do with reading comprehension? Individuals have schemata for everything. Long before students come to school, they develop schemata (units of knowledge) about everything they experience. Schemata become theories about reality. These theories not only affect the way information is interpreted, thus affecting comprehension, but also continue to change as new information is received. As stated by Rumelhart, "schemata can represent knowledge at all levels-from ideologies and cultural truths to knowledge about the meaning of a particular word, to knowledge about what patterns are associated with what letters of the alphabet. We have schemata to represent all levels of our experience, at all levels of abstraction. Finally, our schemata are our knowledge. All of our generic knowledge is embedded in schemata" (1980. 41).

All knowledge is formed in this way but is limited to the experiences we have already stored as memories. The more varied memories a person has, the greater is their ability to mix and match these memories, build or add to a schema to examine new and novel ideas. Of course, this will also require other skills and (social skills such as morals and ethics) related to the ability to imagine, integrate a new and novel new concept. This ability is present in each of us to a greater or lesser degree. It is also related to the ability of that person's mind to be curious enough to attempt to conceptualize the thought in the first place. There are certain people gifted with the ability to recognize new concepts about the knowledge that has never been seen before. There are many fields in which this is true but the uniqueness of the new concept becomes rarer as the endeavor becomes more obscure or novel.

Einstein's revelation that matter and energy are but different sides of the same coin comes to mind. No other mind had ever conceived of this possibility and so, it was completely novel.

How did he even imagine this might be the case? Einstein was one of the most curious people who ever lived. He was not a good student in his early educational life. It is historically known that he did not receive a professorship upon graduation, so he took a job as a clerk in the local patent office. Here he had solitude and time to think. It was his incubator. It was during this time that he wrote his first scientific thesis:

In 1905, seen by many as a miracle year for the theorist, Einstein had four papers published in the *Annalen DEQ Physik*, one of the best-known physics journals of the era. Two focused on the photo-electric effect and Brownian motion. The two others, which outlined $E = MC2$ and the special theory of relativity, were defining for Einstein's career and the course of the study of physics. https://edu.glogster.com/glog/experiment-7002/27bta1j3c50

He was uniquely adept at what is called "mind experiments." He would literally picture a situation in his mind's eye, so he could "see" abstract states. In one experiment, he wanted to find out what would happen if he could ride a light ray chasing another which stared just before he did. Using this mind experiment he found that he could never catch it. He explored beyond standard thinking for a reason, and he found, based on earlier work, that since mass and energy are the same things, as he increased speed the energy being expended was converted to mass, thus it took greater and greater amounts of energy to move his ever-growing mass. It turned the energy, needed to propel his new mass to light, speed had to grow to be infinite and therefore he could never catch the initial light ray which was mass-less. This was a stunning discovery that could not have been figured out by using conventional thinking.

This new knowledge was not a function of assembling prior stored memories into a new configuration. He did use his memories regarding mass and energy, but it was his completely novel approach to putting his mind in a novel situation that led to the discovery. To resolve the deeps problems, one has to be creative and flexible in their thinking. Every great discovery had, at its roots, creative unbounded mind capable of saying maybe it's not this way at all but perhaps … For the sake of clarity and historical accuracy, Einstein reached his intellectual horizon when he refused to embrace a new science, he helped in creating, QP. One of the most important attributes of QP is its inseparability from randomness. He was not able to accept the idea and famously said, "God does not play dice with the universe." This belief ended his progress in the world of new physics. His classical view is still an endpoint of the macro world, but he self-exiled himself from the new frontier of the micro world and quantum mechanics. It is important for you to know that he did not reach his intellectual limit but elected not to accept that there was more.

I have said in another chapter that I do not believe we can stop learning. However, I do believe that we can talk ourselves into stopping, or worse, some institutions or persons might be able to convince us that such and such is true or not true, and we shall never question them. If this happens to run in the opposite direction, question everything. It seems that humans have an inexhaustible ability to learn information and then integrate it with other skills and achieve "true knowledge" after all.

THE UNITY—THE SOURCE OF EVERYTHING

...we will grasp the central idea of it all as so simple, so beautiful, so compelling that we will say to each other, Oh, how could it have been otherwise? How could we have been so blind for so long!

—John Archibald Wheeler (1911–2008)

$$U = \frac{1 \times 1}{\infty}$$

THIS IS THE FINAL CHAPTER OF OUR JOURNEY. IN IT, I will pull all the previous discussions together into one unit of understanding, so that each chapter can be understood as part of an integrated whole. It will be the most esoteric of all you have read. By way of some explanation, let me lay out some overarching themes and a few ground rules. As a convention, I am going to use the words "the Unity" in place of God. This is my way of differentiating the traditional God for something equal but broader in conceptualization.

"The Unity" is one of my own inventions, no doubt a strange one, but I believe it is accurate in light of all we have examined. As you read this, please be mindful, we have covered a lot of temporal, geographical territory, and all that is embodied in the whole of those cultures and their collective, histories, customs, beliefs, social structures. I am therefore going to amalgamate these features into one collective reference that I will call humankind or simply human. In all cases where I refer God, I am referring to humankind's belief in an ultimate agency or agencies, and by whatever label or labels have been put upon Him. What you will now read is the culmination of a lifetime's work, "an Opus." In it, I will put forth my own thesis of how the basic fundamental elements of our universe fit together and function as a whole, and I will lay out my concept of the nature of the agency we call God. My view will be a radical departure from what you have heard before, and by and large, I believe the ideas expressed are unique. You will find elements that may be familiar, as I have built upon centuries of religious and spiritual, philosophical, scientific, and legal traditions. The development of my thesis must necessarily include the thoughts of those who have come before me and made invaluable contributions; this cannot be avoided on a subject of such depth. My wish is that what I have added should become clear as you read along. Earlier in the prologue, I had said that I am a self-ascribed spiritual chimera, part Pantheist, Taoist, and pragmatist. I did qualify my statement by expressing that although I practice elements of the Tao, I did not think it went far enough. I would now like to amend and clarify the remark and say that I believe all spiritual and religious doctrines do not go far enough in trying to understand and explain certain seemly unfathomable elements of God and his nature. However, as you will see, I vigorously disagree with this doctrine.

If we try to understand God nothing bad will happen. What other traditions and religions have not done is to understand God intimately, and examine from our perspective what is God's true nature. This is not a trivial statement. Humanity has spent its entire history asking if there is truly a God. I am not addressing the question of if there is a God, but rather what His fundamental nature is. Humankind's ability to understand and learn appears to be infinite. I see no prohibition to understand any part of our total arena, which of course, centers on God and our relation to Him.

We put no limit on our efforts to learn more in any other field. On the contrary, humans are constantly pushing the boundaries of knowledge. Today's fictions and mysteries are tomorrow's frontiers. One has only to step back, pace by pace, through human history, to see the horizons of knowledge that we have steadily ratcheted in the direction of greater knowledge.

As our worldview and knowledge changes and expands, we outgrow old ways, put in place throughout the millennia, to nurture and protect our evolving societies. Nature provides strategies to influence our physical, psychological, and spiritual survival. Our traditional thinking is based on cultural rules and law, plus guidance from religion and spirituality.

It has been said that humans are designed to recognize patterns (a process known as apophenia). We are born problem solvers and convergent thinkers. No problem is unsolvable when we put our minds to it. When we limit ourselves to a particular adverse or limited

AN HONORABLE JOURNEY   IN SEARCH OF TRUTH

line of reasoning, the solution cannot be found. When a problem defies resolution, I have found it is only a matter of perspective that a problem cannot be solved. This means that it cannot be solved the way we are contemplating it. Another looks at the same problem, from a different perspective, and we can see the solution. We need to take a radical step away from our comfort zone and show flexibility. Any problem can be resolved, but human ego and ignorance block the way.

The Concept of God

Let's take a look at the topic in detail. What is the nature of the universe and God, and how are they related? This is a scientific, religious/spiritual, and philosophical quandary.

To understand the basic nature of God, we must understand the fundamental nature of not only God but the universe. If we accept Saint Amsalem's (Anselm of Canterbury in his 1078 work *Proslogion*), he defined God as

That than which nothing greater can be thought "and argued "*that this being must exist in the mind, even in the mind of the person who denies the existence of God that God is the most powerful, most complete entity we can imagine then it is a simple matter to accept this concept is valid if only by definition. In this view, there would be no question of God's existence.* https://sourcebooks.fordham.edu/ basis/anselm-proslogium.asp#CHAPTER%20II

This is a pragmatic viewpoint that delineates the fundamental discussion of whether there is a God, by a definition that all reasonable men can accept. The question assumes that there is a God as defined by Amsalem. As a result, the issue can be stated as "if" there is an agency such as Amsalem describes, we can give it the name of God. Non-believers are hence excluded from the discussion as they do not accept Amsalem's agent as existing.

No religious, or spiritual, or philosophical persuasion prohibits asking this question, though the orthodoxies of conventional belief systems argue that the nature of God is unknowable. My reasoning falls from the logical perception that God must be the ultimate agency and therefore is at the root of all that exists. God then is all-inclusive and encompasses all reality and, therefore, is all truth, and the truth is encompassed within "Existence."

From that perspective, it follows that my hypothesis is that "Existence" and God are indistinguishable. Existence is the ability to, directly or indirectly, interact with all reality. To be sure "Existence" is a *quale* (pronounced kawlay) or objective quality. This would also mean, by extension, that God's characteristics are indistinguishable from pure existence. This, the final frontier, is the threshold where all that is knowable has the property of existence, beyond this point there is nothing, and everything evaporates into an unbounded void.

To some, this may seem like an oversimplified generalization. However, when we think about it, it makes sense that this concept encompasses everything. Whenever we look at a concept, a thought, or a physical thing, it either exists or it doesn't. Non-existence is outside the duality function (we will address this duality function later on). Simply because it is nothing, a non-entity. Therefore, again, God and "Existence" are the same. This is a key point because an understanding of the very nature of God is the issue. I realize that humankind has (in most cases) anthropomorphized God, we humans have given God a human form along with human emotions such as anger, a sense of mercy, love, etc. but aside from these, we need to seriously and soberly assess what an entity as all-knowing and powerful as God would be like. However, since we have elevated Him to the level of a mysterious entity beyond our understanding, we have essentially set up a veil beyond which we cannot see, and, as I observed, we arbitrarily ascribed certain human characteristics to Him because we have no other emotional or logical choice. This may be what we did, but we did it without foundation and merely to fill our need to connect. This sounds counterintuitive to me rather than circular logic. If I remember my Catholic biblical teachings, we were created in His image and likeness, not the other way around.

In addition, all religious and spiritual belief systems say that there is only one God (perhaps with many manifestations). The pantheon of the Gods is filled with lesser gods who are reigned over by one chief god. This is a simple human trait attempting to quantify and infuse the various human-like characteristic into God. Instead of seeing God's characteristics, we see demigods.

Throughout human history, humankind has imbued God (in any form) with unlimited boundaries and abilities. When we distill God's character to one elemental truth, in the absence of all other lesser qualities, God is the very substance of existence. Without God's existence everything would evaporate into nothingness. In my view, only totally distilled, pure, pristine existence can exhibit such quality, and therefore God's basic quality is that He is Existence and everything else is subordinate.

The Arena of Existence

From a scientific standpoint, existence would include time and space as well. Modern cosmology posits that we live in a multiverse, an infinite froth of bubble-like universes. Ours is one of many and is called the local universe since it is the one we live in. For the sake of convention, I will call the multiverse the global universe because it includes our local universe. What can and cannot be done in our local universe has been determined by the laws of God/Existence, which are absolute and woven into the fabric of the local universe. From all we know about our physical universe, it is the rules that govern our universe that is inviolate. If God was arbitrary and caused an exemption to these laws, the fabric of the local universe would collapse in chaos. This point of view is analogous to asking how a vehicle, such as a standard automobile, could continue to function with one wheel removed. This is why there are no miracles in science. The laws which govern our local universe are the essence of why things work the way they do and work in the same way everywhere and at all times. To break even one of these laws would undermine the entire fabric of our reality. This very fact means that these laws create and maintain our universe, and the two cannot be separated.

Physicists over millennia have established our universe's basic operational parameters by certain qualities called "constants" and function across all time and space. Typically, there are twenty-four such constants. Listed below is a diagram showing these constants and their values:

Table of Physical Constants (Revised January 2008)

. Electron rest mass me $9.109 \times 10{-}31$ kg

. Proton rest mass Mp $1.6726 \times 10{-}27$ kg Electronic charge e $1.6022 \times 10{-}19$ C

. Speed of light in free space c 2.9979×108 m s-1

. Permeability of free space µ0 $4\pi \times 10{-}7$ H m-1

. Permittivity of free space 0 $8.854 \times 10{-}12$ F m-1

. Planck's constant h $6.626 \times 10{-}34$ J s

. Reduced Planck's constant h¯ $= h/2\pi$ $1.0546 \times 10{-}34$ J s hc ¯ 197.33 MeV fm

. Boltzmann's constant kB $1.3807 \times 10{-}23$ J K-1 Gas constant R $= kB/mH$ 8.250×103 J kg-1 . . K-1

. Molar gas constant R 8.315 J mol-1 K-1

. Avogadro's number NA 6.022×1023 mol-1

. Standard molar volume $22.414 \times 10{-}3$ m3 mol-1

. Unified atomic mass unit (12C scale) u 931.5 MeV/c2 = 1.660538× 10−27 kg

. Mass of hydrogen atom mH 1.0078u = 1.6735 × 10−27 kg

. Bohr magneton μB 9.274 × 10−24 A m2 or J T−1

. Nuclear magneton μN 5.051 × 10−27 A m2 or J T−1

. Proton magnetic moment μp 2.7928μN

. Neutron magnetic moment μn -1.9130μN Bohr radius a0 5.292 × 10−11 m

. Fine structure constant α = e2/(4π"0hc ̄) (137.04)−1

. Compton wavelength of electron λC = h/(mec) 2.4263 × 10−12 m

. Rydberg's constant R∞ 1.0974 × 107 m−1 R∞hc 13.606 eV

. Stefan–Boltzmann constant σ 5.671 × 10−8 W m−2 K−4 Radiation density constant a = 4σ/c 7.561 × 10−16 J m−3 K−4

. Gravitational constant G 6.673 × 10−11 N m2 kg−2

There are twenty-four fundamental constants. If any of these was changed even by only 1 billionth of 1 percent, or less, our universe would be a wholly different place. These constants are inviolate. Even if God wanted to, He could not change these without irreparably modifying the structure of the physical universe. I have included them so you can try to imagine how finely tuned our universe is.

While faith is tremendously useful in the guidance of human interaction on a spiritual level, any invocation that God plays favorites in the machinations of men, is at odds with reality and how our reality works. So, while we can pray for help from God, He is self-prohibited in meddling in the rules (a rule which He created) of our universe. It doesn't make any sense for God to create such a finely tuned universe only to break His own laws for our convenience. While we can sometimes mistake good outcomes for solutions for the impossible challenges in life as God's intervention, it is more likely that we have not known or understood all the elements which have led to the fortuitous outcomes. Apparent mitigation of the laws was instead pure chance and mistaken for God's intervention. If one insists miracles are real, they are forced to concede that the rules of our universe are malleable, and we know, through science, and through the rule of truth that they are not.

Many statistical tests calculate correlations between variables, and when two variables are found to be correlated, it is tempting to assume that one variable causes the other. That "correlation proves causation," is considered a questionable cause and a logical fallacy when two events occurring together are taken to have established a cause-and-effect relationship. This fallacy is also known as *cum hoc ergo hoc*, Latin for "with this, therefore because of this," and is a "false cause." It is true that there are situations that we do not understand, but this doesn't automatically mean there has been a miracle. This means that we don't understand everything there is to know.

Does this mean that we should not pray? Of course not! Prayer brings us hope and comfort and this in itself is consistent with an arena of life where hope is a valuable survival tool. Seen in this light, religion, spirituality, and my thesis are entirely compatible with the concept of God as pure Existence. Along with universal laws of existence, the evolution of the "natural" social laws for human conduct is wholly natural and compatible. The existence of preeminent God (the ultimate agency) is very compatible with truth. This assertion is as valid as any religious, spiritual, philosophical, or scientific point of view.

The Gordian Knot and God

If we are to understand the relation between Truth and God, and ourselves, we must venture deep into depths that transcend our temerity regarding the nature of God. I have tried to explain that there is no prohibition that prevents us from focusing on this question. Our first course of action is to allow ourselves to go beyond the old outdated barriers that keep our mind prisoners to a forbidden inquiry. I have reconciled with myself that I am a devoted spiritualist, but I am also a pragmatist. Therefore, I reject, as I hope you will, any notion that any entity, as powerful and all-knowing as God, would prohibit us to explore all regions to gain knowledge. As others have named their God or the supreme entity, I have named the ultimate reality in my belief system "the Unity." This is appropriate because a unity is a single entity that encompasses all that exists. The rules of logic and the tenets of spiritualism and religion, philosophy, and science are also compatible with the pure existence that I call the Unity.

The Unity encompasses all. The Unity is an analog for what you would call God. It is all there is and has no beginning and no end. This is a simple concept to understand when framed in a familiar setting much like a ring that has no beginning and no end. Therefore, when asked where a ring ends and begins, we see that the question is simply meaningless. There was never a temporal coordinate called the beginning for the Unity, and so as far as time is concerned, there will never be a beginning or an end.

In our day-to-day reality, we can look to Einstein's relativity equations and see for ourselves that the flowing of time is an illusion that our consciousness creates to make sense of the way we perceive time as past, present, and future. Relativity has proven, beyond a shadow of a doubt, that the only time that exists is the "now" moment. The Unity exists now, at a singular moment that has no past and no future. It exists here at this place and there are no other locations. Such coordinates as space and time are qualities that are a function of our local universe, and the Unity encompasses the local universe and all other universes which exist. The place "here" is eternal as all time is only one moment and is infinite. Time and space in the local universe are illusions. As in the traditional view of heaven and hell, these are not physical locations, but states of mind created by our belief system. In reality, they are illusions.

The rules of the local universe have built-in illusions that are real to us, living in a temporal and location-bound universe. This is consistent with concepts within the Tao and other Eastern spiritual belief systems. The Unity also dovetails well with quantum theory's non-locality.

The Duality Paradigm and Tension

The concept of the Unity also holds that there is only one entity of which all else is a subordinate part. This means at the Unity level there is no duality as there is in the local universe. In our universe, we have a built-in duality such as up-down, dark-light, wrong-right, male-female, etc. Every place we look at we will find duality, it is ubiquitous. My conjecture is that the dynamic tension between physical and non-physical duality-based entities is the mechanism of action that animates the local universe. This is the fundamental force that supplies the push and pulls moves to all things. In other words, this basic pull–push tension is what animates our local universe and gives it its energy. Duality is embedded in our universe; it is present everywhere in our concept of time (i.e. now and then). There are other examples of forces at work which we do not usually encounter in our day-to-day experience. For example, did you know empty space has vacuum energy? Vacuum energy is underlying background energy that exists in space throughout the universe. This behavior is codified in Heisenberg's energy-time uncertainty principle. Still, the exact effect of such fleeting bits of energy is difficult to quantify. The vacuum energy is a special case of zero-point energy (ZPE) that relates to the quantum vacuum. ZPE is the difference between the lowest possible energy a quantum mechanical system may have and the classical minimum energy of the system. Unlike classical mechanics, quantum systems constantly fluctuate in their lowest energy state due to the Heisenberg uncertainty principle. The result is that the seemingly empty space is not a perfect vacuum as we normally imagine.

Below is an example of tension in practical use. Buckminster Fuller was a futurist and inventor of the twentieth century who worked in the field of tension mechanics. Below is a structure that is constructed from cables and poles. Note that none of the poles touch each other, and yet the structure stands independently. This is an example of the power of tension and shows that tension can operate when their physical structures do not connect.

Things are quite different when dealing in the realm of the Unity. Here, there is no duality, only one point, and is powered by the innate tension created within the process of existence itself. It is its own source of energy.

The equation below is the philosophical representation of the formula to express the Unity.

$$U = \frac{1 \times 1}{\infty}$$

The Unity is equal to 1 multiplied by 1. This yields 1, thereby collapsing the duality function to 1. This 1 is then divided by infinity and yields 0. So, we see a Unity is equal to infinity or an entity without end, and by extension has characteristics all of which are infinite. This would be an entity or agent with unlimited capability except for which it places on itself.

Remember, this is not a mathematical equation but a philosophical one, used to illustrate how duality functions in our local universe can be neutralized, and the product can then be set to yield infinity. A Unity is an infinite result which is what is desired.

Concepts Within the Unity

In an ultimate reality of pure existence, all things are reduced to one point. If we extend this to Eastern philosophies, all substance disappears as does the concept of time expressed as a continuous flow from the past to the present and on to the future. Time is an illusion useful in the local universe but meaningless in the concept of the Unity.

Time and space in the local universe are completely woven together. Time is the "when" dimension. Time happens when we seek a temporal coordinate to navigate to an event or when we ask the temporal distance between two or more physical locations such as "how much time does it take to travel from Los Angeles to New York?" Space is the medium between (in quantum loop gravity theory, space is actually an elastic field constructed of quanta (bits) of gravity) locations. These locations can be of any length. Such as the example given earlier or between one side of the galaxy and the other, or the distance between the nucleus of an atom and its electrons. In essence, this is what is at the root of non-locality and quantum entanglement. This leads to the conclusion that all elements of the Unity are folded into one entity.

The Unity is, by our standards, completely alien, precisely because it is characterized as an infinite single entity, and therefore time and space are meaningless. As a result, time and space do not really exist. These qualia (time and space) are reduced to a single coordinate "now/here." In other words, there is only one continuous moment that stands in place and does not flow, and only one place which is here and never anywhere else.

Since we are creatures of the local universe, we cannot conceive of a place so alien. If we try to reach out with our imaginations, we must invent situations outside our concepts and outside our experiences.

The Nature of God/Unity

Since our beginnings, humans have sought to understand and define why we exist. I could claim with some certainty that our spiritual selves contain some latent memory of the original concept of a creator (though neuroscientist has looked for a God gene but have not found one) which ties us to the Unity (God) though He exists in a different reality.

Traditionally, all Gods do not live in our corporal world. In Islam, Allah is in paradise, for Christians He is in heaven, each spiritual or religious worldview has its word for heaven. My view is no different. We do not lack the ability to invent names for our Gods, mine is the Unity. In the end, it doesn't matter, the concept is essentially the same. However, I should draw the distinction that the Unity and "Existence" are inseparable, and they exist everywhere which is here/now.

I also believe that our brains fill in the blanks with ideas from our copious imaginations when we run into dead-ends and when the physical world does not yield the answers we seek. These answers take the form of our myths centering around our belief systems. I, myself, found that I longed for a spiritual connection with something greater than myself. I needed an entity with whom I could personally communicate, but after rejecting all the religions and spiritual systems, I decided to do what everybody else does, I invented my own. I know most of us don't need to invent their own spiritual guide. Most of us inherited it from our parents, culture, or by a personal search among the vast variety readily available. I did not have that option. However, in order to be consistent with my own belief system, I created an avatar which is a stand-in for the Unity.

I know this is just a creation of my mind. I do believe in the Unity, my avatar (an avatar is the embodiment of a person or idea) is something I can connect with spiritually, as you do with your God. I did not feel comfortable with a God who needed to be prayed to or held a standard in which I could not feel a mutual bond with, so rather than creating a father figure, I created a brother figure. A relationship more on an equal plane.

I also have the advantage of being part Taoist, so my brother instructs me, while in meditation, to seek answers from myself, dig deeper into my own mind, and look for ideas that are novel and creative but also resonate with who I feel I am. This is basically the teaching mode of Taoism and is called *Direct Pointing*. In this school of thought, a master will never provide a clear-cut answer to your questions but will provide something for you to consider and leave the learning up to you. So, to do this, I provide my own answers, knowing that my avatar (through mediation) asks me to look deeper and consider other options. This works for me.

All of this boils down to your personal belief system. I prefer to leave mysticism behind and see my belief system more practically as in philosophy and science. I also leave servitude behind; my brother and I are part of the Unity, which is the whole of reality, in a very real way we are part of everything and by the doctrine of "the whole is the sum of its parts" all part has the same value and we are equals in the Unity. There is no hierarchy in our relationship, we are more like partners in the whole of reality so, this means that I have the same value as the Unity.

CONCLUSIONS

I REALIZE THAT MY CONCEPT BREAKS SHARPLY WITH traditional religiosity and spirituality, but I believe it is closer to reality. It has the property of removing an interceding deity and makes anyone adopting this point of view directly and absolutely responsible for themselves and their actions. By extension, I do not consider myself subject to external forces or circumstances that affect my ultimate outcome. I can either accept this responsibility or not and the consequences of my action or inaction lie squarely on my shoulders.

Though I do not have the concept of sin, and thus no hell, I feel a heavy self-imposed responsibility to do no wrong. This responsibility is strictly between me and the Unity. Whatever I choose, because I try to make my choices based on wisdom and because they are right, lead to an honorable path. However, being human I do understand that I sometimes fail. This why the acquisition of wisdom and the ridding of the ego is so much a part of my life philosophy and is essential. I also accept that I am completely subject to the rules of the local universe which does not allow externally created dogma by humankind such as divine intervention or miracles. There are the absolute rules of the local universe and the social customs of humans and what I call the natural law which excludes harming.

The concept of the Unity is almost, but not quite, the same as the concept of God, the Tao, Brahma, Amaterasu, Allah, Jehovah, or countless others. But, as I indicated earlier, my take on the teaching about these Gods does not go far enough. They do not tell us anything about the actual nature of God, only the names of some of His characteristics. This would be like describing an apple by its color and texture and weight or shape alone, you would still not know the essence of the apple. I feel we can learn more. As a result of this philosophy, I have a clearer concept of the nature of God/Unity.

However, I have to admit that for the past several years, I have been stalled concerning the concept of the type of cognition the Unity has. This is a difficult question. Cognition is not fully understood in humans. Recent studies on both animals and plants indicate that some do have a type of cognition. Certainly, we are aware that dogs, birds, dolphins, and tortoise, and octopus are intelligent. Plants do not have brain cells, but research has shown that they do react in specific survival modes to stress and, in some cases, can convey this stress to neighbors via chemical transmitters. But when I think of an entity on the grand scale of the Unity or God my mind freezes. The only cognition we can experience is our own, so when we think about God, we naturally anthropomorphize Him. However, this is a trivial viewpoint and can't be right because it is "not big enough." Such a thing as God, if He has a mind like ours, would be so much larger (or simpler) that we could hardly imagine it. Maybe God's mind or whatever we would call it is so alien to us that we are incapable of imagining it. Perhaps the Unity is self-aware without the need for a mind as we know it.

I was about to give up on this subject but after a short meditation, I came upon a new way of looking at the problem. It occurred to me that everything in our universe is animated by some set of instructions or hidden codes. What code, for example, tells our eyes to see. The act of vision lies in a relationship with the light hitting the eye and transmitting a coded neurological image to our visual cortex where it is translated into an image (of course this is a gross simplification of the entire process). This appears to be automatic but what causes this scenario to initiate the interaction between light and our eye, and where does the code that controls this action lies even if it is switched on all the time. There are examples of this type of animation every-where we look.

It appears to me that the entire universe, and all its components, runs on some code that animates it; this "calls it to action." Whatever this code or set of instructions is, it is ubiquitous. To me, it seems self-evident that something must be a prime mover getting everything going and keeping it going. I can't help but wonder if this is the cognition of the universe (the Unity) at work. Once the breath of life sparks when the sperm penetrates the egg, a chain of instructions and codes cascade into action which causes the newly formed cell to split, again and again, finally forming a new child. But what causes life to come into existence. We are immediately persuaded to conclude that it's a miracle, but maybe it's not. Maybe there is a reason that life happens which is not divine. When we boil water the tumultuous action of the water is not caused by a divine act, it's caused by the water becoming heated by some external source, it's becoming altered thermally. Everything we know happens for a reason, it is true that sometimes we don't understand the reason, but given enough time and effort, we have a long history of unraveling great mysteries.

In my present state of mind, I am happy to put this new concept into the crucible of filters I use to scrupulously vet all new ideas. Ultimately, I am satisfied with my concept of the Unity. The idea is more satisfying than being trapped in a world where I am not allowed to think that I can know more about the ultimate reality and its nature. I am satisfied to feel that I am part of something so inspiring and all-encompassing that it is not divine but natural. It's not hard for me to imagine that when I die, the basic atomic elements of my corporal being will just mingle with the fabric of the Unity. That, I feel, should be enough for anyone.

After reading this, you may cynically think that I have just come full circle to the traditional concept of God, but you would be wrong. I feel that, at least for myself, I have demystified the concept of God as mankind has traditionally conceived of Him. The Unity is much more than the traditional God. The idea of the Unity attempts to reconcile religion, spirituality, philosophy, science, and metaphysics in a way that has not been done before; this concept dissolves the duality of our local universe and ties all reality together using spiritualism, philosophy, and science as a foundation. Here you will find no complete reliance on faith and no concept of mysticism.

Now, a final word about my credentials for putting this spiritual/ philosophical theory forward. I would point out that among the history's greatest religious or spiritual worldviews have been put forward by my predecessors who had no greater credentials than I. Buddha, Christ, Lao Tzu, Zarathustra, Mohamed, and many others. They did not possess any academic credentials or honors imparted on them, yet they established great schools of thought that have been elevated by time and devotion to worldwide belief systems. While I claim no such exalted position, I would appreciate the same respect accorded anyone who takes the time to seeks truth and a novel way of giving life meaning.

I will continue my honorable journey to wherever it leads me, and hope that you will get some measure of knowledge and insight from what is contained herein.

> *...we will grasp the central idea of it all*
>
> *as so simple, so beautiful, so compelling that we*
>
> *will say to each other, Oh, how could it have been*
>
> *otherwise? How could we have been*
>
> *so blind for so long!*

EPILOGUE

Mystery has its own mysteries, and there are gods above gods. We have ours, they have theirs. That is what is known as infinity.

—**Jean Cocteau** (1889–1963),

I WOULD LIKE TO THANK YOU FOR TAKING THE TIME TO read this book. At times, it may have been tedious. The last chapter is esoteric and not always easy to understand. This is not because it is mysterious, but because I have proposed a rather alien concept outside the norm of typical thinking.

The purpose of committing my thoughts to words was born of my personal desire to a lifetimes journey to clarify what I learned along my journey, and leave a bit of knowledge for those who thirst for more than what the traditional, religious, and spiritual belief systems provide.

Additionally, I have been looking for an endpoint, an answer to the age-old question about an ultimate creator or force which animates our universe and all we know. What I found was not God, but a condition of suchness which is much larger and more beautiful than I ever imagined. I did not find an authority figure or a Being who lords over us, but I did find a force of unimaginable simplicity and tranquility, that has what we would call "absolute wisdom," which can guide us back to ourselves, to figure things ourselves.

In this view there is no judgment of us, so much as there is an arena which we call life where we are left to discover our own destiny. Here, we are guided only by our own human rules of cultural conduct or the simple, straightforward laws of nature, plus the physical laws of our universe. The Unity does not require anything of us. If we choose, we may take part in its essence which is the natural flow of existence and harmony as a foundation for living our lives.

The structure I chose for the book was to walk you through the basic steps I hoped would lead to a solid foundation, on which to discover a novel view of the most fundamental understanding of what reality is actually like. To do this, as I know from my own journey, you had to have a solid logical footing that would help clarify what you could believe in or discard. The subjects covered were intended to give you just an introduction to those foundation stones. You could spend your life, as I did, to tease them out for our human collective knowledge and experience.

In any event, it is my sincere wish that I added to your search for truth. My final admonition, to anyone who wants to take their own journey, is to have patience, gain ever more wisdom, rid yourself of the ego, and always practice self-discipline. I have included a free verse poem I penned one day when I was seeking to release myself from my own ego but retain a spirit of a vibrant life in which I could still contribute.

"Who am I?"

I am the sound of a storm telling you that I am coming.

I am the cry of a baby calling to its mother.

I am the slow movement of a snail sliding across the rusted gate latch.

I am the drift of haze above the morning forest.

I am the kiss of lovers on their first night alone.

I am the cadence of the waves which break on timeless shores.

I am the cool breeze that lifts that pretty girl's skirt in Amsterdam.

I am the tears of joy of a new mother holding her baby.

I am the glazed eyes of a fallen soldier the moment after his soul has fled.

I am the first star you see at twilight and the last at morning light.

I am the warmth of the sun that falls on you from the sky in summer.

I am the smell of good food as you pass me on a Paris boulevard.

I am the soft wind made by the wings of a passing butterfly.

I am love of children for each other as they play in the park.

I am the hushed sigh of the rain outside your window.

I am solitude and sorrow and the longing wish for tomorrow.

I am the one who waits for you to wake in the morning.

I am without end.

I am

I am

I am I am no one.

SOURCE

Dixit, Avinash K. *Lawlessness and Economics: Alternative Modes of Governance.* Princeton: Princeton University Press, 2017.

Stanford Encyclopedia of Philosophy. "The Coherence Theory of Truth." Stanford Encyclopedia of Philosophy, June 26, 2018.

Peirce, C.S. "The Collected Papers of Charles Sanders Peirce." Edited by C. Hartshorne, P. Weiss (Vols. 1–6), and A. Burks (Vols. 7–8). Cambridge, MA: Harvard University Press, 1931–58.

Sperberg, Dan. "David Hume, the anthropologist, born May 7, 1711." The International Cognition & Culture Institute (ICCI), May 7, 2011.

Dawkins, Richard. "Don't Force Your Religious Opinions on Your Children." *Time,* February 9, 2015.

Wikipedia. 2020. "Buddhism and Violence." June 12, 2020. https://en.wikipedia.org/wiki/Buddhism_and_violence

Wikipedia. 2020. "Mahabharata." June 14, 2020. https://en.wikipedia. org/wiki/Mahabharata

BBC. "Buddhism at a Glance." Accessed November 17, 2009. https:// www.bbc.co.uk/religion/religions/buddhism/ataglance/glance. shtml

Wikipedia. 2020. "Existentialism." June 14, 2020. https:// en.wikipedia.org/wiki/Existentialism

Holloway, April. "Australian Aboriginals - Creation Myth." Ancient Origins, March 18, 2013.

McCoy, Daniel. "The Creation of the Cosmos." Norse Mythology for Smart People, n.d.

Wikipedia. 2019. "Mesoamerican Creation Myths." https:// en.wikipedia.org/wiki/Mesoamerican_creation_myths

Pagans Origin of the Christ. "Glycon Shows the Ideas Behind Pagan Religion." Pagans Origin of the Christ, n.d. https://pocm.info/ pagan_christs_Glycon.htm

Suratwala, Shabbir. 2011. "Born of a virgin, Isis." Facebook, July 3, 2011. https://www.facebook.com/GSHMP/photos/a.244967 038862064/244967075528727/?type=3&size=333%2C450&f bid=244967075528727

Murdoch, D. M., and Acharya S. "Attis: Born of a Virgin on December 25th, Crucified and Resurrected after Three Days." Stellar Home Publishing, n.d. https://stellarhousepublishing.com/attis/

Boucher, Tim. "Dwyfan and Dwyfach (Welsh mythology)." Tim Boucher, October 18, 2019. http://www.timboucher.ca/2019/10/dwyfan-and-dwyfach-welsh-mythology/

Wikipedia. 2020. "Self-organization" June 5, 2020. https://en.wikipedia.org/wiki/Self-organization

Simpson, David. *German Aesthetic and Literary Criticism.* Cambridge University Press, 1985.

Haken, Hermann. "Self-organization." Scholarpedia, 2008, 3(8):1401. http://www.scholarpedia.org/article/Self-organization

Pigliucci, Massimo. "What is Wisdom?" Medium, February 13, 2020. https://medium.com/@MassimoPigliucci/what-is-wisdom-8a2f1a611dbd

Lee, Michelle. "Yes, U.S. locks people up at a higher rate than any other country." *The Washington Post*, July 7, 2015. https://www.washingtonpost.com/news/fact-checker/wp/2015/07/07/yes-u-s-locks-people-up-at-a-higher-rate-than-any-other-country/

Ryan, Julia. "American Schools vs. the World: Expensive, Unequal, Bad at Math." *The Atlantic,* December 3, 2013. https://www.theatlantic.com/education/archive/2013/12/american-schools-vs-the-world-expensive-unequal-bad-at-math/281983/

Etehad, Mellisa, and Kyle Kim. "The U.S. Spends More on Healthcare than Any Other Country — But Not with Better Health Outcomes." *Los Angeles Times*, July 18, 2017. https://www.latimes.com/nation/la-na-healthcare-comparison-20170715-htmlstory.html

Stockholm International Peace Research Institute. "Global Military Expenditure sees Largest Annual Increase in a Decade— says SIPRI—Reaching $1917 billion in 2019." Stockholm International Peace Research Institute, April 27, 2020. https://www.sipri.org/media/press-release/2020/global-military-expenditure-sees-largest-annual-increase-decade-says-sipri-reaching-1917-billion

US Department of Agriculture. "Food Security and Nutrition Assistance." US Department of Agriculture, September 12, 2019. https://www.ers.usda.gov/data-products/ag-and-food-statistics-charting-the-essentials/food-security-and-nutrition-assistance/

Summers, Lawrence. "Trump claims credit he is not due on the economy." *Financial Times,* August 6, 2018. https://www.ft.com/content/493f20de-9959-11e8-88de-49c908b1f264

Wikipedia. 2020. "Reality." May 21, 2020. https://en.wikipedia.org/wiki/Reality

Wikipedia. 2020. "Existence Precedes Essence." March 27, 2020. https://en.wikipedia.org/wiki/Existence_precedes_essence

Falk, Dan. "What is the multiverse?" NBC News, May 22, 2018. https://www.nbcnews.com/mach/science/what-multiverse-ncna876136

ABOUT THE AUTHOR

Bob Alba has been writing poetry for fifty years. Her has won Best Poets and Poems of 2122 Award thorough the Word Poetry Movement. He has also published two espionage books, love story and one book of Haiku style love poems. He is a lifelong senor member of the American Society for Quality and a Manufacturing Engineer. Bob has been and industrial product designer for many years and his products have been sold across the world. He has founded five corporations. He is also a graphic designer and photographer. He now is the Director of Operation for Lynne Alba Speech Therapy Solutions, P.C.

He lives, works, and writes in Long Brach California and can be reached at bob@childspeech.net.